A JOURNEY TO THE KINGDOM SERIES

INTRODUCING

THE KINGDOM

YOUR BASIC GUIDE TO UNDERSTANDING THE KINGDOM OF GOD

Introducing
THE KINGDOM
YOUR BASIC GUIDE TO UNDERSTANDING THE KINGDOM OF GOD

Dr. Dana Carson

Dedication

I want to first dedicate this book to my wife and friend, Rachelle Dianne Carson and our wonderful children, Dana II, John Anthony, Angel Naomi, Marielle Alli, and Devon Jarrod for their unending sacrifice of me as their husband and father for the betterment of others.

This book is also dedicated…

To my staff who supports all of my ministry endeavors: April, Bertreece, Cherrice, Danielle, Fred, Jermaine, Jerohn, Julia, Katrin, Raul, Shannon, Tanya, Tiffiny, and Tyrus.

To my sons in ministry: Pastors Charles Moody, Louis Straker, Samuel Johnson, Chris King, Nathan Roberts, Eugene van Kramburg, William Kettor, Mishael Carson, and Sechaba Mothiane.

To The ROCK church family, thank you for sharing me with the world!

Contents

Foreword

W e are in the dispensation of the Kingdom of God. While Christ ushered in the presence of the Kingdom among men, the abandonment of the message of the Kingdom impacted contemporary thought concerning the Kingdom. Through the process of Romanization and colonization, the message of Christ and His Kingdom has been greatly misunderstood and neglected. The message of the Kingdom is the end time message based upon Matthew 24:14 that implies that the message of the Kingdom will be preached throughout the world and then shall the end come. Many ask the question today, hasn't the message of the Kingdom been preached for centuries? Unfortunately, due to Romanization and colonization, the message of the Kingdom has not been preached in its purest form due to the dispensational process and prophetic seasons. This book is designed to provide for you a solid understanding of the Kingdom of God and is the first of a series of books written to assist the Body of Christ in understanding and embracing Christ's message of the Kingdom of God. This book is written as a sequel to three of my other books on the Kingdom of God: *One True King, The Doors of the Church Are Closed, and Lord Help! I'm Trapped in the Church.*

The Kingdom of God is what you and I would see according to John 3:3 and would enter into according to John 3:5. The Kingdom pre-requisite was conversion according to Matthew 18 and was to be sought after as life's number one priority according to Matthew 6. My commitment and prioritization of the Kingdom message has existed for over a quarter of a century. The call of the Kingdom has led me to begin the Kingdom Lay Bible Institute (KLBI) where those who are interested in receiving comprehensive and affordable Bible training with a Kingdom emphasis can do so both on multiple site campuses and online.

I also host an annual Kingdom Summit and Symposium that focuses upon varied aspects of the Kingdom of God. The Summit and Symposium is presented by three Kingdom scholars: one Greek scholar, one Hebrew scholar, and me. The other two presenters are full-time seminary professors at a world class seminary where I also do some adjunct professorship in leadership.

I have also written a Kingdom education curriculum that is designed to teach and train Kingdom disciples on the fundamentals of the Kingdom. My Kingdom call also led me to begin a Kingdom Five-fold School of Ministry (KSM), where the five-fold ministry gifts can be trained online and on-campus. My commitment to the Kingdom is far more than a fad, but a calling; thus, I have a number of teaching and preaching resources to equip people to grow in Christ and His Kingdom. This book will prove to be beneficial to the reader and their quest to understand and embrace the Kingdom.

Chapter One:
The Kingdom

We are living as believers in a very strange season and context. Being a Kingdom citizen today is not very popular; however, certain types of church attendance are smiled upon. The majority church in North America today has adopted the values of the greater society and its politics. We have moved from the apostolic to the democratic; thus, most major decisions made in the world and in churches are by popular vote. While as a natural citizen I believe in the democratic process, as a Kingdom citizen, I believe in a theocratic process. God is sovereign, He is the King of His Kingdom!

When Christ came in the 1st century, He came into a political climate that was familiar with royal dynasty and imperial rule. The Roman Empire was controlling most of the so-called civilized and developed world. While Judaism existed as the only monotheistic faith of the day, philosophy was considered the highest form of intelligence and wisdom. Thus, Aristotelian and Platonic thought flooded the Greek and Roman world in the form of gnosticism. It was believed that the material world was evil and the immaterial world was good and the goal of the individual was to escape the material or physical world through higher thoughts and reasoning. It was this kind of world in which God was made flesh or material and dwelt! What a contradiction of thought and practice! The divine *logos* or knowledge of God became material. Dr. Carson, where are you going with this? I'm simply trying to establish that the Kingdom is, and always has been, a counter-culture expression. So as we begin to teach you the Kingdom, it will oppose your flesh and will present an upside down view of life.

When God invades or enters into the world of humans through His transcendency, He does so to transform those who are willing to follow His Kingship! Hence, whenever He enters in, He must transform and cleanse those who will become His servants from the stains and residue of the civilization that He has come to transform them from.

Think about it, He pulled Noah and His family from the society and cleansed them through the flood; He called Abraham away from His family and developed he and his sons. He pulled Joseph aside and worked with him, and ultimately Moses and Israel. Then, in the New Testament, we again see the call to come out from among them and be separated! The point is God is a God of transformation, and He raises up people that He can use to impact their generations during their lifetime.

You and I are called to impact a 21st century global community through the preaching, teaching, and demonstration of the Kingdom in a highly technical context. In a technological society, people are not easily impressed when they see amazing things due to the amazing potential of technology. While technology appears to be responsible for the saving of lives and longer life spans, it is not a miracle, even though technology is doing some pretty amazing things through I-technology and beyond. We have incredible vehicles, war machinery, and computer technology that blows the mind.

Technology simply taps into the amazing potential of the natural world that some brilliant minds and dreamers dared to think possible. Many of the technological devices that we can no longer live without came from people imagining the invisible world of technology, like sending messages through the airwaves. It is simply amazing how fast wireless connections transports messages from Facebook, Twitter, and visual imagery through Skype and 4G technology. Just think about it – the world believes in unseen technology and puts complete trust in it through human ingenuity, but denies the power of God. You can see how people believe that with technology who needs God anymore?

The amazing and the supernatural have been around for quite some time from the building of the pyramids to the power of magicians and witchcraft. When Christ entered into our material world, He did so supernaturally.

God the Father transported His divine Seed (*spermatos*) to an ovulating virgin, and it fertilized her egg, causing her to conceive the promised Messiah, Christ, who entered a counter-culture in a miraculous way in order to bring a shift in how a relationship with God should function.

God desires to shift the church into a Kingdom posture and this involves the church being willing to be counter-culture not culturally affirming. This is a tough job when we consider that the culture has in some ways been good to all of us; we still enjoy some of its benefits and offerings. So the first move of God was He took us out of our comfort zone, the way we were accustomed to thinking and behaving and took us through the wilderness. This move allowed us to be deprogrammed from the world's way of thinking. Thus, the Bible states, "Let this mind be in you which was also in Christ Jesus", and "be transformed by the renewing of your mind". The Kingdom message and power is the only means of transformation that is present to transform a person. However, this has always been the fact from the beginning. Thus, when the plan of God's redemption unfolds in what we refer to as the New Testament, it does so with the preaching of a message that we don't see in the Old Testament scriptures – the Kingdom.

The New Testament begins with Christ the Messiah or He that was born King of the Jews (Matthew 2:2, 11). The New Testament message begins with the birth of a King, and the first message in the New Testament is the message preached by John, the baptizing one. John's message was "Repent!" or "Change the way you think; get your head ready for revolution for the Kingdom of God is ready, are you?" So after over 400 years of God being silent, He now spoke through a very unlikely figure who was very counter-culture to the practicing clergy. Matthew, the synoptic writer, quotes the prophetic voice of Isaiah and characterizes John the baptizing one as "the voice of one crying in the wilderness: Prepare the way of the Lord; Make His paths straight".

John's message of the Kingdom was so counter-culture that one required baptism in order to be qualified as a disciple or follower of John. John, however, was very intentional to ensure that his hearers and followers understood that he was simply a forerunner, not the point of focus. He contrasted himself with Christ and stated that he was not worthy to carry His sandals.

The proclamation of the Kingdom of God was Jesus' central message as seen in the synoptic gospels – Matthew, Mark, and Luke. In Luke 4:43, Jesus said He must preach the Kingdom of God. In Matthew 4:23 and 5:20, the Sermon on the Mount, as it popularly known, is concerned with the righteousness that qualifies people to enter the Kingdom of God. Further, the entire teaching on the Mount, Matthew 5-7, is what I term 'The Constitution of the Kingdom,' with its preamble – the Beatitudes. Matthew 5:3-11, the collection of parables in Mark 4, and Matthew 13 illustrate the mystery of the Kingdom of God, which has been entrusted to us (Matthew 13:11, Mark 4:11). Matthew 26:29 and Mark 14:25 show the establishment of the Lord's Supper and looks forward to the establishment of the Kingdom of God.

The message of the Kingdom was first introduced to the 1st century people and then the New Testament reader. What was this message of the Kingdom? Why did we not see it in the Old Testament? Some people believe that the Kingdom of God is a New Testament phenomenon. However, God was present in the Old Testament Hebrew scriptures as the King of Israel. When Miriam wrote her song after the deliverance from Egypt and the crossing of the Red Sea, she wrote, "Our God reigns" (Exodus 15:18). God is King and stated that He will make Israel a kingdom of priests (Exodus 19:6). It is clear that God is presented as King in the majestic or royal Psalms, as well as the King sitting on the throne in Isaiah 6.

The message of the Kingdom became clearer, however, during the intertestamental period, or the 'between the testament' period, due to the persecution that the Jewish people suffered, under the leadership of a man named Antiochus Epiphanes (mad dog), who desecrated the temple of Israel and profaned the things of God. They believed that the only way that God could fulfill the prophecy that the throne of David would have no end, He would have to overturn the evil world. Thus, the phrase or concept "the Day of the Lord" emerged. This concept was believed to be a time when God would totally obliterate evil and turn the world over to the rulership of Israel under God – the fulfillment of the restoration of the throne of David. Even though temple worship was done away under Israel's domination by foreign powers, they maintained their faith in God. It was during this period that the religious sects, such as the Pharisees, Sadducees, Essenes, and Qumran community emerged. This was the time when synagogues were developed, due to the destruction and defilement of the temple, and worship was moved to a smaller context. These developments did not exist in the Old Testament.

It is really important to understand the historical context for the Kingdom message in order to understand some of the New Testament text. Some of the beliefs of the Messiah were created during this period. The coming King and Messiah would come with healing, power, and deliverance in order to restore all things back to Israel according to the prophetic throne of David. Thus, the expelling of demons, healings of sickness and disease, and power over death were all thought to be signs of the Kingdom. The day that God overpowered evil was thought to be the Day of the Lord or the coming of the Kingdom. Prophetically, John the baptizing one came preaching the Kingdom, Christ came preaching the Kingdom, the disciples were commanded to preach the Kingdom, and the 70 were sent to preach the Kingdom. The mission of the church was, and still is, to open the gates of the Kingdom, not the doors of the church!

Some people have asked me as I travel the world preaching and teaching the Kingdom, "What is the difference between the Kingdom of God and the Kingdom of heaven?" While some have very ignorantly developed doctrines on the differences, there are none. Matthew's gospel frequently uses the term "Kingdom of heaven", while Mark and Luke always use "Kingdom of God". "Heaven", in these instances is a circumlocution – a way of referring to God without using His name, which Jews and Jewish Christians believed too holy to pronounce or even write.

Matthew was a Jew, who greatly esteemed and reverenced the decalogue commandment, "You shall not take the name of the LORD your God in vain". In fact, the Jewish scribes and copyists took this commandment so literally that they would not write the name of God in a way that it could be pronounced. When copying the scrolls, every time they came to the name of God *Yahweh*, they would remove the vowel markers to make it impossible to be pronounced. This is called, in academia, the tetragrammaton (YHWH). When writing the name, they would drop their writing utensil and say *"ha shem"*, which means, in Hebrew, "the name". So when you read Matthew's gospel, he tends to stay away from the phrase "Kingdom of God" and prefers to use the "Kingdom of heaven". Mark and Luke tended to use "Kingdom of God", they were Gentile writers who didn't have that strict background of the Ten Commandments. So when reading the New Testament, please do not make the mistake of thinking that there is more than one Kingdom or a kingdom different from the one about which Christ taught. There is only one Kingdom to be sought (Matthew 6:33), entered into (Matthew 18:3), and one to see (John 3:3).

The book of Acts opens with a discussion of the Kingdom in chapter one and ends with Paul preaching and teaching the things concerning Christ and the Kingdom of God.

The early church, while being the custodian of the Kingdom of God, was under tremendous persecution as it assumed the responsibility of expanding the Kingdom throughout the world. Christ gave the apostles the mandate to take the message of the Kingdom to the uttermost parts of the world (Acts 1:8).

Life in the 1st Century

In the 1st century, Rome ruled the Mediterranean area, known as Palestine, where Jesus was born and lived His life. In accordance with Roman law, the Jews were allowed to be fairly self-governing, but were under the authority of a local ruler, Herod, who reported to the Roman Emperor – Caesar. When Rome recognized any religion, its god was simply added to the official Roman pantheon. The Romans used this as a means of allowing its conquered peoples to maintain cultural identity, while also identifying themselves nationally as Roman citizens. In Rome, you were allowed to worship in any manner you so desired with one exception. All Roman citizens had to recognize and honor Caesar as God above their provisional and regional religious god(s). Because Christians claimed the exclusivity of Christ and His message as the only means of knowing and interacting with God, Christianity's God did not fit in the pantheon nor could Christians be relied upon to exist peacefully in the midst of religious pluralism.

Since Judaism was the religion of Palestine and Christianity was an off-shoot of Judaism, Rome recognized it as a legal religion. During the first two decades of its existence, Rome tolerated its presence, seeing it simply as one of several Jewish sects. However, by the time the Apostle Paul was placed on trial, Rome considered Christianity an illegal, divisive religion that could be easily targeted for persecution and/or elimination because of the Christians' adamant and staunch position regarding the exclusivity of Christ – even at the threat of harm or death.

Christian Persecution and the Kingdom Message

The persecution of the Christian church began during the reign of Nero (54-68 AD), who started a trend of Christian persecution that would last until the 4th century. In 64 AD, Rome suffered a large fire that burned throughout the city for six days and seven nights, consuming three-fourths of the city and resulted in widespread economic devastation to the Roman economy. It was believed that this fire was set by Nero himself, who, according to legend, fiddled while the city burned. Historians record that in order to avert attention and suspicion from himself, Nero used the fledgling Christian community as a scapegoat, accusing members of the local sect of starting the fire in an attempt to overthrow the empire. What followed was nearly 250 years of cruel and torturous punishment of the Christian community at the hands and permission of the Roman government.

Christians were fed to hungry wild animals; dipped in tar and set on fire; mauled by wild bulls; doused with wax and used as human torches at sporting events; nailed to crosses, beheaded, and rolled down hills in spiked barrels. These atrocities became so commonplace and widespread that the surviving members of the once bold and thriving Christian community were forced underground into hiding in order to preserve their lives. As a result, the Kingdom message could no longer be spread. Instead, it was shared among the secret gatherings of believers.

While the abolishment of Christian persecution provided an era of peace for the 4th century church, it also created a context for compromise. The Edict of Milan (313 AD), signed by the Emperor Constantine the Great to stop the persecution of Christians, ended the formal era of Christian persecution. Constantine the Great, not only abolished Christian persecution, he declared Christianity the official religion of Rome.

Constantine made this decision based on a dream he had that inspired him to place Christian symbols on the shields of his soldiers. His dream led him to believe that if he did this, they would win their battle. So, Constantine followed his dream, won his battle, and Christianity became the official religion of Rome. It must also be noted that Constantine also saw the political advantages of making Christianity the official religion of Rome.

The legalization of Christianity began an era called the Patristic period where emerging scholars of the faith began to write and attempted to define the faith. Great men, like St. Augustine, Athanasius, Cyprian, Ambrose, Origen, the three Cappadocians, and others began attempting to standardize the faith with orthodox beliefs. Out of this period came the great creeds and doctrines of the faith, such as the Nicene Creed and the Creeds of Constantinople, Ephesus, and Chalcedon, as well as the doctrines of Christ, Holy Spirit, and the Trinity.

During this period, however, the merger of Christianity and the Roman Empire also began and led to the merger of paganism and Christianity. Various pagan celebrations and offices were simply changed over to Christian celebrations, though they had pagan roots. Many of the official celebrations of the contemporary church have their foundation in Eastern mysticism, even those we hold dear to our hearts, such as Christmas and the like. Please read my book *"The Doors of the Church Are Closed"*, and it will give you greater insight on some of the historical events that have taken place and shaped the contemporary church.

During His time here on earth, Jesus declared that although the Kingdom had been repeatedly attacked by its adversaries, it (the Kingdom) had been relatively silent. Christ further stated that during His ministry, the Kingdom would no longer suffer violence or any hostile attempt to overtake it (Matthew 11:12).

However, take a survey of the modern church and it will quickly become evident that something went terribly wrong as the Kingdom message made its way from the 1st century to the present day. As a result, the modern church is all but devoid of understanding of Christ's Kingdom.

The Kingdom Message Held Captive

Christ's ministry was inaugurated in order to make known, first to Israel and then the Gentiles, the will of God according to the rule of God. Christ was consumed with conveying the message of the Kingdom of God. He lived His life to explain its culture and the necessity of entering and living within its boundaries and according to its parameters. Although the primary focus of Christ's ministry centered around proclaiming, explaining, and demonstrating the Kingdom of God, some 2000 years later, the church world is only now, just beginning to gain a foundational understanding of His Kingdom message.

What began, as a vibrant reformation in the Jewish community through the preaching and teaching of Christ and His disciples and eventually the conversion of the Gentile world largely through the efforts of the Apostle Paul, came to an abrupt end in the face of extreme and vicious religious persecution. Thus, while Christ's message of the Kingdom is the most overarching and prevalent subject found throughout the synoptic gospels (Matthew, Mark, and Luke), today, it is difficult to distinguish between fake Kingdom rhetoric and the truth of the Kingdom as presented by modern pulpiteers. Its true meaning and significance to the Body, both now and in the coming eschaton, are understood by only a very small percentage of the five-fold ministry and, even fewer, lay persons. As such, despite this recent resurgence of interest in the Kingdom message, a substantive discussion of its character, structure, and citizens has been largely non-existent within the church. Its definition, placement, and purpose will vary widely based upon who you talk to.

- *Word of Faith* followers describe the Kingdom as both the surest means to, and the supplier of, health, wealth, and prosperity.

- *Dominion theologians* consider the Kingdom of God to be the source of a new world order by which sin on the earth will be permanently overturned and God's people will be given access to natural power and authority.

- *Liberation theologians* see the Kingdom manifested largely in terms of political and social change.

- *Charismatic theologians* associate the Kingdom of God with manifestations of the power of God evidenced in tongues, healings, and power over demons.

Christ and the Kingdom of God

Ambiguity concerning His Kingdom was certainly not intended by Christ who stated emphatically in Luke 4:43 that the purpose for which He was sent was to preach the Kingdom of God. The Kingdom of God was the principal cause for which Jesus lived and died. Appearing over 100 times in the New Testament, the Kingdom of God was the last topic of discussion Jesus had with His disciples before His ascension (Acts 1:3). Luke concludes Acts with Paul "preaching the Kingdom of God and teaching the things which concern the Lord Jesus Christ" during his two-year confinement in Rome (Acts 28:31).

Christ was inundated with the Kingdom of God and lived His life to explain the culture of the Kingdom and the necessity of being part of the Kingdom. During His three-year ministry, Christ taught the following regarding the Kingdom of God:

- The Kingdom of God is spiritual – John 4:24
- The Kingdom is to be valued above all else – Matthew 13:44-45
- The Kingdom must be sought out – Matthew 6:33
- You must be born again to see and enter the Kingdom – John 3:3-5
- The Kingdom is redemptive and causes men to repent – Matthew 21:32
- The Kingdom is multicultural – Matthew 13:47
- His Kingdom is not of this world – John 18:36
- The mysteries of the Kingdom is privileged information – Mark 4
- The Kingdom is a present and future reality – Matthew 10:5-7; 12:28

Christ's Kingdom teachings were carried out through the use of parables – natural illustrations that were used to explain the spiritual character and content of the Kingdom of God. Utilizing the rabbinic tradition of proclamation, explanation, and demonstration, Christ utilized the revelation of God to make the message of the Kingdom of God and its existence plain to the disciples. By preaching, Jesus declared the message of the Kingdom of God; by teaching, He explained its meaning and character; by healing and miracles, He demonstrated its presence and power in the world. The Kingdom of God was clearly the highest order man could aspire to and being a citizen of God's Kingdom was the greatest privilege made available to humanity.

Defining the Kingdom of God

So exactly what is the Kingdom of God and what is its importance to modern believers? Is the Kingdom of God of any substantive importance or simply a representative paradigm by which to understand the historic structure and functions of His heavenly and earthly administrations?

The answer to these questions has occupied the thinking of theologians and scholars for years. Thus, the Kingdom conversation does not come without a great amount of controversy.

The Kingdom – The Possession of the King

The Greek word for "king" is *basileus* and is defined as "a sovereign invested with supreme authority and power to rule over a designated people." Linguistically, the word "kingdom" is a compound word derived from two root words – king's domain. Kingdom refers to "the domain or dominion of a king"; domain refers to "the territories that are under a person in ultimate authority". The term "Kingdom of God" translated into Greek is *Basileia tou Theou*. This term speaks of the Kingdom as being God's possession and designates it as the place where God is recognized as the supreme, unquestioned ruler.

Righteousness, Peace, and Joy

Romans 14:17 also provides insight on a formal definition of the Kingdom of God. Here, the Apostle Paul states that God's Kingdom is righteousness, peace, and joy in the Holy Spirit. These three words represent states of being that should define and characterize the life of a person who has confessed Christ as Lord and entered God's Kingdom.

The Greek word for "righteousness" is *dikaiosune*, which means "justification or right standing". In the Hebrew language, righteousness is translated as *tsedeq*, which means "to be right with God". Romans 3 tells us that Jesus became our righteousness, and we were declared righteous through Him! Thus, in order to be in the Kingdom of God, one must first be declared righteous based upon his/her confession of the finished work of Christ. Then through forgiveness, we are reconciled and no longer exist in an adversarial relationship with God – we have peace, which erupts in joy!

The Greek word for "peace" is *eirene*, which means "oneness, quietness, rest, set at one again". The righteous positioning we receive as a result of our confession of Christ as Lord reconciles us into right relationship with God the Father. Becoming one again with the Father encourages feelings of peace, security, safety, prosperity, and felicity among all Kingdom citizens. The Greek word for "joy" is *chara*, which means "cheerfulness, calm delight, or gladness." Joy is the disposition that should characterize the life of all Kingdom citizens due to the relationship of peace we enjoy with the Father as a result of being declared righteous by Christ.

The Kingdom of God is best defined as "the rule of God in the hearts of men who submit themselves to the sovereign will and plan of God for their lives". Having been declared righteous, these men and women now exist in a peaceful relationship with God and experience the joy of a loving relationship with the King that is characterized by humility and service.

Where is the Kingdom of God?

While the theme of the Kingdom of God has been the topic of discussion in many seminary classes around the globe, to date, this discussion has not been communicated to the church with any depth. Scholars have debated the question, "What did Jesus mean when He discussed His Kingdom?" The prevailing discussion in the schools of theology is the debate over whether or not Christ's Kingdom is a part of active history or if it merely pertains to the end times. While emphasizing the end times message of the Kingdom as an important aspect of the Kingdom of God, C.H. Dodd focused upon its present reality. He is known for his concept of realized eschatology, which depicted the future power of God manifested in the present ministry of Jesus. Still others, such as G.E. Ladd in *"Inaugurated Eschatology"*, attempted to define the Kingdom by arguing the presence of the future.

He suggested that the Kingdom that will come has already begun acting upon the hearts of men and establishing the reign of God until the fullness of the eschatological manifestation. However, regardless of the emphasis used by these scholars, they all agree upon one thing. Each states that the Kingdom is here, but not in totality – an argument born out in New Testament scriptures.

Matthew 10:5-7 states:

> *These twelve Jesus sent out and commanded them saying: "Do not go into the way of the Gentiles, and do not enter the city of the Samaritans. Go rather to the lost sheep of the house of Israel. And as you go, preach, saying: 'The kingdom of heaven is at hand.'*

Matthew 12:28 which reads:

> *But if I cast out demons by the Spirit of God, surely the kingdom of God has come upon you.*

and Luke 17:20-21 which reads:

> *Now when He was asked by the Pharisees when the kingdom of God would come, He answered them and said, "The kingdom of God does not come with observation; nor will they say "See here" or "See there!" For indeed, the kingdom of God is within you.*

The Kingdom is Near You

The answer to the question "Where is the Kingdom of God?" is derived as follows. The Kingdom of God is *entos humon* or "in our midst". In other words, the Kingdom exists around us, but cannot be perceived by natural means. As believers, we experience the Kingdom of God when the effects of the Adamic nature and its genetic transfer to all mankind are overturned. Thus, the Kingdom of God is the realm where the power of God overturns the power of Satan and the results of the fall of man. We, believers, are the geography of God.

His Kingdom exists anywhere the hearts of men have been subjected to His holy will and seek to bring it (His will) to bear similarly in the lives of others.

Resident within the placement of the God's Kingdom is an explanation of its purpose. What is the purpose of God? The ultimate purpose of the Kingdom of God is to, once and for all, overturn and eradicate the effects of the fall of man on mankind, the physical earth, and all living creatures. What is the position of the Kingdom of God? It stands in clear opposition to the kingdoms of this world. Satan dominates this age, but God will usher in the "age to come" and began that process with Jesus' inauguration of the Kingdom message.

Still wondering about the structure of the Kingdom of God? Still asking yourself the question "How do I enter God's Kingdom?" If so, that's perfectly understandable. Let's take one last look at the Kingdom of God by looking at the components that must be present in order for a kingdom to exist in the natural world. Three components go into establishing a kingdom. Those components are:

What Makes a Kingdom a Kingdom?		
Component	Definition	Scripture Reference
King	One who rules with authority	John 1:49
Subjects	Citizens	Ephesians 2:19, Philippians 3:20
Realm	The kingdom proper – its natural parameters and geography	Matthew 6:10

King

What is a king? Thomas Oden, a professor of theology from Drew University defines it as follows: "a *basileus* is a sovereign invested with supreme authority, that he may rule over a certain people, according to just laws, that he may have power to reward the good and punish the evil, and that he may defend his subjects, not having anyone superior to him." Christ is the King of kings, prophesied about by Isaiah (9:6), saying the government would be upon His shoulders.

Subjects

A kingdom consists of citizens who are born in it. Likewise in the Kingdom of God, Kingdom citizens are "born" into the Kingdom (John 3:3-5, Philippians 3:20, Ephesians 2:19). Romans 10:9-10 states the following:

> *...that if you confess with your mouth the Lord Jesus and believe in your heart that God has raised Him from the dead, you will be saved. For with the heart one believes unto righteousness and with the mouth confession is made unto salvation.*

Thus, the heartfelt belief in and confession of Christ as Lord, is the means by which admittance to God's Kingdom is obtained.

Realm

Christ is the King of God's Kingdom and the realm over which He has been granted divine rule and authority is the whole earth and everything within it. His realm is also manifest in the hearts of the men and women who subject themselves to His rule and seek His throne for their deliverance (salvation).

Chapter Two:
The Kingdom and the Church

The two most important institutions to God are the church and the Kingdom of God. The relationship between the Kingdom and the church is inextricable. The Kingdom is the rule of God, whereas the church is the human community under that rule. Unfortunately, most contemporary Christians see themselves as members of the church and not people of the Kingdom. Today's church, as a sociological phenomenon, is defined by race, class, denominationalism, and several other 'isms'. Because of this interpretation and perpetual practice of the church, many have abandoned the idea of church, and others are simply ignorant of the church. Most people are aware of the concept of church, but are ignorant concerning the church and its relationship to the Kingdom of God, even to the point of thinking that they are synonymous. The message of the Kingdom has been sabotaged by the sociological concerns of those who desired to gain cultural supremacy and financial advantage, because the church is interpreted as the final authority of God. But the church was birthed through the Kingdom. The principles of the Kingdom were designed to govern the activities of the Kingdom through the church. Thus, the Kingdom is the supreme organization of God that conducts its business through the church.

Though the theme of the Kingdom is clearly found throughout scripture, and has been discussed in many seminaries, to date, its preaching and teaching have not been the emphasis of the Christian church. Indeed, many churchgoers are so ignorant of the concept and expression "Kingdom of God"; they believe that "the church" and "the Kingdom of God" are interchangeable terms that refer to the same entity. However, this is not the case, and an examination of the scriptures will help us as we attempt to define the Kingdom, describe its culture, and identify its King.

The Church and the Kingdom of God

And this gospel of the kingdom will be preached in all the world as a
witness to all the nations, and then the end will come – Matthew 24:14

The word "gospel" is the Greek word *euaggelion*, which comes
from the combination of two terms: *eu* meaning "well or good",
and *aggelos*, which means "message or new". Thus, in this scripture,
Christ is saying that the message of the Kingdom of God is good
news to those who hear it. However, until recently, the message of the
Kingdom of God has been one rarely heard preached from pulpits
across North America. Instead, the messages we commonly hear are
those which promote an individual's loyalty to the church to which
he or she belongs. Messages preached in the church have resulted
in believers who identify and are very comfortable with the culture
of their church, but are oblivious to the culture of the Kingdom.
Don't misunderstand me please, I believe in commitment to the
local church, but I have seen people who would rather die before
they would not be a part of their church, a church that left them
with very little knowledge about the Bible. The local church must
be committed to the principles and government of the Kingdom.
People have belonging commitments to churches that satisfy what
Abraham Maslow would deem belonging needs, which is one of the
three deficiency needs of all humans according to his research and
theory. It is dangerous to be committed to organizations that are not
committed to Kingdom principles, which are found in the scriptures.

With such an emphasis being placed on church by contemporary
Christians, one would believe that this was the emphasis of Christ's
ministry. However, this is not the case. The word "church" is only
recorded three times in the gospels – once in Matthew 16 when
He formally declares the establishment of the church, and twice in
Matthew 18 when He instructs the disciples on conflict resolution
among believers in the church.

> *And I also say to you that you are Peter, and on this rock I will build My church, and the gates of Hades shall not prevail against it. – Matthew 16:18*

> *"And if he refuses to hear them, tell it to the church. But if he refuses even to here the church, let him be to you as a heathen and a tax collector. – Matthew 18:17*

On the other hand, the word "kingdom" is referred to more than 100 times in the New Testament. It is the most over-arching topic stated in the synoptic gospels, and as such, warrants that a significant amount of attention and study be devoted to understanding it.

Matthew 16:19 gives us insight into the relationship that is supposed to exist between the church and the Kingdom of God. The scripture says:

> *And I will give you the keys to the Kingdom of heaven, and whatever you bind on earth will be bound in heaven, and whatever you loose on earth will be loosed in heaven."*

Christ builds – *oikodemeo* – His church (*ekklesia*). *Oikodemeo* comes from the Greek word *oikos* which means "house or habitation". Thus, Christ is saying He will exist inside or inhabit the church. The word "church" in Greek is *ekklesia*, which is a compound word derived from the words *ek* meaning "out" and *kaleo* meaning "called, to invite, to summons" and has the implication of selection.

What is the Make Up of the Church?

The church is made up of those individuals that have been called out, invited, or summonsed for the service of the Kingdom. The term *ekklesia* is a political term that centers on the gathering of a cabinet. So when we talk about the church we are talking about a gathering of a cabinet of representatives. Thus, the church should literally function as an embassy (to be discussed later).

The church must be a reflection of Christ's Kingdom on the earth. Christ stated that He placed the keys to the Kingdom of God under the jurisdiction of the church. He gave the church the responsibility of allowing people entrance to the Kingdom and to serve as the mediator between them and the world. In short, the church is the custodian of the Kingdom. The church was not intended to be the focus of the people of God; it was simply to be a vehicle that was to be used on behalf of the Kingdom of God.

The problem is that the church has become a sociological phenomenon. Instead of representing the unified Body of Christ, the church has become segmented and divided based upon racism, classism, sexism, denominationalism, and other kinds of schisms. The church is a very divided institution, and each local church represents the majority culture of those who are a part of it, rather than representing the agenda of the Kingdom. Consider today that the Sunday morning eleven o'clock hour is still the most segregated time in America. It is the time when diversity cannot be enforced as it is in work environments; people are free to choose where they will worship. When people are left to their own, they tend to worship in their own cultural context. There have been efforts to integrate. However, note that almost all of the diversity or integration work in the church has been directed toward encouraging minorities into the majority culture worship rather than the majority culture accepting the invitation of minority culture churches. This is a spiritual travesty, because this disregards the fact that God has called and raised up a multicultural representation in the Body of Christ. Since colonization, people only work on diversity into one environment, the majority race.

The church is not the Kingdom when we have white churches, black churches, Korean churches, Latino churches, etc. There is only one Kingdom – the Kingdom of God. The church must experience a renewal of commitment and vision of the Kingdom.

If you are reading this book, God is calling you to a perspective renewal – you are not a church member; you are a Kingdom citizen. It is impossible to enter the Kingdom without the church. We must regard ourselves as Kingdom citizens who are part of the church; born in the Kingdom, but called to work through the church. The Kingdom and the church were intended to exist in a symbiotic relationship – separate but bonded together. The Kingdom gave birth to the church, and the church is now accountable to the Kingdom. Neither can accomplish its goal without the other; however, the Kingdom can exist without the church, but the church cannot exist without the Kingdom.

The Kingdom is Not the Church

The Difference Between the Kingdom and the Church
Have you ever heard of the phrase, "majoring in minors and minoring in majors"? It means that the focus is on the wrong thing – the less important at the expense of the all important. Imagine if a mother discovered that her son had taken a neighbor's property, and upon confronting her son she chastised him for bringing stolen property into her home: "Don't you ever bring stolen property into my home again; now go to your room!" What's wrong with that response? The son is still free to steal as long as he finds another hiding place. This is what the church of Jesus Christ is guilty of today – focusing on the wrong thing. Over the course of the last 1,500 or so years, what started out as the message of the Kingdom of God has become the message of the church. It has caused two vastly different types of Christians to emerge depending on which message is the focus.

The counter-culture of the message of the Kingdom began with John the baptizing one. While mainstream society's religious circles were one way, John was in the wilderness crying out about a concept that was misunderstood and neglected: the Kingdom of God.

He prepared the way for Christ, and when Christ came He also began to preach that the Kingdom of heaven is at hand. So if John the baptizing one preached the Kingdom of heaven and Jesus preached the Kingdom of heaven, why after 2,000 years, are we preaching "church?" The topic of the Kingdom of God has been one of the most misunderstood and neglected topics in scripture, with the majority of saints still extremely unclear about the function and nature of the Kingdom of God. In Matthew 6:33, Jesus commanded us to "seek first the Kingdom of God and his righteousness and all other things shall be added unto you," but how do you seek that which you do not understand? If we neglect what God tells us to prioritize, then how can we truly be in His will? Of course, you cannot "seek" what you do not understand, and God will not add all other things if we neglect what He wants us to prioritize. Accordingly, when we examine most contemporary Christians, it is no surprise that they have become so entangled in the contemporary church that a true understanding of the Kingdom of God is absent.

What is the Church of Today and Why is it Like it is?

The church has become a sociological phenomenon that is predicated upon race, class, sex, and other kinds of 'isms.' So, rather then reflecting the Kingdom of God, the North American church is dominated by culture and reflects that culture. In the Kingdom, the church was intended to be a vehicle used on behalf of the Kingdom of God, not a place that focuses on the people! However, the problem is that people love the church, because it reflects the natural mentality of the people, rather than the mentality of the King. Stated another way, in America, we love the church, because it is predicated upon the culture and governmental practices of democracy where, as a republic, we function based on the principle of "majority rule." When such a principle is applied to God's church, the strongest personalities in the church tend to govern things – regardless of what the scriptures may dictate.

In the church, many times the persons making decisions, whether it be a board or by congregational vote, do not have to know the scriptures, do not have to be anointed, or really even possess a Bible to be honored as one of the leading authorities in the church. The church, like our government, is viewed as belonging to the people and their natural hue. Their cry is "more power to the people!"

The problem with the way that we have embraced and practiced very democratic principles in the church is that the Kingdom of God is a theocracy. It is a place where God himself rules through His ordered authority, and He does not care about our vote, our decisions, and how we may feel about it. This concept is foreign to us, and we tend to perceive this kind of rule negatively. Our flesh naturally embraces the concept of "majority rule", because it is what we are familiar with and what we are used to functioning in. Our democratic mentality has been ingrained in us through our educational system, and we are firm in the idea that the democratic process is the way in which justice in our nation is achieved. In North America and many other places throughout the world, we only understand the church of the people, for the people, and by the people. We love this church, because it has become the haven for us to protect our cultural and ethnic uniqueness. However, there is no such thing as church based on race, class, or sex; there is only one church and it is the Body of Christ that reflects the Kingdom of God on earth.

Today's contemporary church is akin to a group therapy center where the focus is on people's wishes and desires. We no longer come to hear the King's instructions to us, but come to hear a word for ourselves. We hear these statements all the time:

- "I'm looking for a church that meets my needs"
- "I'm looking for a church that makes me feel comfortable"
- "I'm looking for a church that makes me feel 'at home'"

God's Word says this earth is not our home (1 Peter 2:11, Hebrews 11:13), thus we should not feel at home. In the Kingdom, we are supposed to attend church to get a Word from the King, but because that is no longer our focus, name-only Christians no longer make an impact on the world. How can we impact the world when our attendance is not connected to the all powerful King? The focus is inward, not outward to a dying world. Quite simply, most people's relationship with God is self-centered, masked in spiritual terminology and Christian tradition.

Statistics are very alarming and suggest that the North American church is declining very rapidly, numerically. Some statistics suggest that it takes 85 Christians in the course of an entire year to win one convert, compared to other religions that are growing, and compared to Christianity abroad, which is also growing.

A Crucial Moment in Time

We are in a prophetic moment where a changing of the guard is occurring – a transition – from the church back to the Kingdom. To use a biblical paradigm, think for a moment of the familiar story of David and Saul. David was anointed to be king and through him, God would usher in the strongest monarchial rule that Israel had ever seen. But it did not happen overnight. David was anointed king in the desert as a shepherd boy, but he did not assume the throne for a period of about 25 years. When he was anointed, that which was to come later was not in place but in transition, and while it was in transition he was not acknowledged or recognized as king. Saul, who was the existing king, had a son named Jonathan, who was the best friend of David. Saul represents tradition and the "people's choice"; Jonathan was in between tradition and that which was new, and David represents that which was new and was "God's choice". Currently, the church is in a position where it must deal with a departing 'Saul', who is no longer anointed to take the church/people of God to the next level.

In the middle of the old and the new, there are bunches of 'Jonathans', who have to decide whether they are going to die with their father 'Saul' in the wilderness, or live in the new with 'David'. If you are going to live with 'David', there is going to be a process. Just like with David, it will not be a popular process; it is going to cause some pain, some tribulation, require sacrificing, and entail some suffering. We are in transition in this prophetic season, and we have to learn how to have an ear to hear what God is saying to His people. It's time for a change in the Body of Christ.

Though people complain about the church, few are willing to change it. The majority of the critics of the Christian church are church folks! Yet most of the negativity associated with the church comes from us. We have too many church folks and not enough Kingdom citizens. Today, more then ever we need power – power which only emanates from the Kingdom, not the church. Truly, our focus must be redirected toward those things that Jesus emphasized and not what we ourselves have created.

Chapter Three:
The Church as the Kingdom Embassy

God's Need for an Embassy (2 Corinthians 5)

Let's take a closer look now at the role and importance of the church. If the church is not supposed to focus on church membership – what is the call and purpose of the church? In this chapter, we will examine the concept of church in its most comparable analogy – the embassy of the Kingdom. Let's look at Paul's writing to the church at Corinth.

> *For we do not commend ourselves again to you, but give you opportunity to boast on our behalf, that you may have an answer for those who boast in appearance and not in heart. For if we are beside ourselves, it is for God; or if we are of sound mind, it is for you. For the love of Christ compels us, because we judge thus: that if One died for all, then all died; and He died for all, that those who live should live no longer for themselves, but for Him who died for them and rose again.*

> *Therefore, from now on, we regard no one according to the flesh. Even though we have known Christ according to the flesh, yet now we know Him thus no longer. Therefore, if anyone is in Christ, he is a new creation; old things have passed away; behold, all things have become new. Now all things are of God, who has reconciled us to Himself through Jesus Christ, and has given us the ministry of reconciliation, that is, that God was in Christ reconciling the world to Himself, not imputing their trespasses to them, and has committed to us the word of reconciliation. Now then, we are ambassadors for Christ, as though God were pleading through us: we implore you on Christ's behalf, be reconciled to God. For He made Him who knew no sin to be sin for us, that we might become the righteousness of God in Him." – 2 Corinthians 5:12-21*

"Reconciliation," "the ministry of reconciliation," "the word of reconciliation" are a few of the terms that are prominent in the above scripture. These terms help us define what we as the church are supposed to be doing. The concept of ambassador carries a special meaning, as well as, the ministry of reconciliation in our modern society.

First, what is reconciliation? A look at this word "reconcile" or "reconciliation", in modern vernacular, will only tell us part of what we need to know in order to gain a deeper insight into the church through this passage. According to Merriam-Webster Dictionary, "reconcile" means "to cause to be friendly or harmonious again; adjust or settle differences; to bring to submission or acceptance." The KJV New Testament Greek Lexicon defines the word as follows: "to change, exchange, as coins for others of equivalent value; to reconcile (those who are at variance) return to favor with, be reconciled to one to receive one into favor." But what you cannot look up is the context and the culture that surrounds these terms. We may know what the word "reconcile" means, but not know the cultural context in which it was spoken. So we will have to delve into the scripture and understand the cultural context in which it was spoken or else we will not understand what the writer is saying. In order to really hear the Word, one has to hear it contextually.

Paul said that we are ambassadors and have been given the ministry of reconciliation. It is as though God is pleading through us for those around us to be reconciled with Him. It is so important that we understand what God is saying so that we will understand the need for an embassy. Paul writes these words from the basis of a theocratic mentality vs. a democratic mentality. A theocratic mentality means that God governs through sovereign authority vs. the process of democratic voting. Contrasting the two is a real study in opposites. In a democracy, things are decided by the people's votes and what they think is fair. Things are very political and subjective. In the natural, we live in the context of man-made laws, freedom of speech, and of the principle of the majority rules. The Kingdom operates on a totally different basis than a democracy. For example:

- In the Kingdom, there is a sovereign ruler; there is only one king.
- In the Kingdom, God is just, not fair (Deuteronomy 32:4).

- In the Kingdom, leadership is appointed, not elected and there is justice, not classism, racism, sexism or any other "ism".
- In the Kingdom, there are no man-made laws, but God-given laws.
- In the Kingdom, one does not have "freedom" of speech; one must watch what they speak or not speak at all. James 3 lets us know that a Kingdom person cannot say what he or she desires to say, because the tongue matters.

As believers, we are now a Kingdom people. As Kingdom people, when we give our hearts to Christ we no longer belong to ourselves. In order to get saved, you must first call Him King. This very familiar Pauline epistle to the Romans is one that demands that we acknowledge Christ as King as a pre-requisite of salvation. Romans 10:9-10 says:

> ...that if you confess with your mouth the Lord Jesus and believe in your heart that God has raised Him from the dead, you will be saved. For with the heart one believes unto righteousness and with the mouth confession is made unto salvation. – Romans 10:9-10

As a result of our salvation, we are under the monarchial rule of Christ. The above verse says, "if you confess with your mouth the LORD Jesus". "Lord" in the Greek is the word *kurios*, which according to the KJV New Testament Greek Lexicon means "he to whom a person or thing belongs, about which he has power of deciding; master, lord the possessor and disposer of a thing, the owner; one who has control of the person, the master in the state: the sovereign, prince, chief; a title of honor expressive of respect and reverence, with which servants greet their master; this title is given to: God, the Messiah."

You cannot have a relationship with God unless it is predicated upon Him being the sovereign ruler and you being the servant.

How you see God determines how you see yourself, and how you relate to God determines how you relate to life.

When Paul says to confess Him as *kurios*, sovereign, master, Lord, that means your life is now without options. When you come to God, you give up your rights. If you want to have an option-driven life, a socially approved life, Christianity is not for you. Oh, you say, but what about free moral agency? Well, you have a choice, but you do not have a right. Your choice will bring about guaranteed consequences. Anything that involves a consequence is not a right. You have a choice not to get saved, but you do not have a right not to get saved. If you possessed the right to not get saved, you could enjoy the same outcomes and benefits as others who chose God. So, you only have a choice.

Because most of us do not understand a theocracy, largely because of the vast differences in our modern democratic cultural context compared with that of the biblical cultural context, we do not know what authority and submission is. And since we do not know, we are confused about the entire structure and plan of God. Paul demonstrates that he understood by calling himself a "bondservant" or slave of God. If we do not understand sovereignty, we cannot understand servanthood. If we do not understand that He is sovereign, then we cannot understand that we are servants. That is the reason so many people do not consider themselves servants of God and they consider themselves volunteers. A volunteer in a democracy has a right to participate or not to participate. But in a theocracy, one must relate to the Lord as His servant. All rights are gone, and the servant exists to execute His will. A servant must now submit to the authority of the Lord. When you awake, say, "Lord, what do You have for me to do today, who do You want me to talk to, give to, or perform an act of kindness for today?" Only then can you say you are now on a mission for the Lord and under full submission to my Lord.

...for in Him we live and move and have our being, as also some of your own poets have said, 'For we are also His offspring.'' – Acts 17:28

In today's culture, people generally have a negative perception regarding submission because of the low regard people have for most levels of authority. As a leftover from the 60s, most believe that authority should be questioned, challenged, and, of course, not blindly followed. Why won't this way of thinking work in the Kingdom context?

Once we jump the cultural baggage we have learned to attach to the terms 'lord, servant, sovereign and submission', we are in a position to hear what Paul is saying in 2 Corinthians 5:12-21. Paul outlines the position of a believer in relationship with God, which is the same as one who serves his king in a foreign territory. When Paul said he was an ambassador, he was saying that he is working through an embassy. He's a representative from a foreign land. Thus, Paul teaches us that the mission of a Christian is to represent His sovereign ruler and His sovereign's interests in foreign territory. As Christians, we are on assignment. We are on a mission for God! As soon as you gave your life to Christ, you died and then He sent you back to the natural world as His representative. Your life is now governed by your submission to the Lord who has sent you here on assignment.

When you give your life to Christ, God sends you straight to the church, which is His embassy. The church should be a reflection of God's Kingdom in heaven. The King disperses us into the embassy/church to serve, which is called the pillar of truth. So it is a place where people can come to be educated about His Kingdom to learn how to enter in! When we understand the language Paul is using about ambassadors and ministers of reconciliation, we know that he is talking about being sent from a foreign place and representing His sovereign ruler in order to spread and perpetuate His interests.

In order for Christ to live in you, you must die to yourself, which means there has been a switch in your life's mission. That means your vision for living changes. You are now supposed to exist for the will of God and willing to allow Him to make His plea of reconciliation to the world through you.

Therein lays the importance and need for the embassy: we come to the embassy to get trained for our mission. There are two types of people in an embassy, ambassadors and ministers. The ambassador is the head of the local embassy and those who serve under him are ministers of foreign affairs. If you are born again, you are a minister, and you should have a ministry. How can you have a mission without a ministry, and how can you have a ministry without a mission?

The ambassadors are appointed by the King for the equipping of the ministers for the work of ministry. The Greek word used to describe what he does is *katartismos* or "equipping" (Ephesians 4:11), which is the breaking or setting of a bone in place. When He can break you to place you, you can be anointed. The ambassador has a place for you in the embassy, and God will break you to place you where you can be used and be your most effective. You cannot become a servant until you have been broken or placed for efficient usage. This takes place in the embassy. The ambassador should be equipping you for your mission. Everyone who is saved should be on a mission. This is why it is necessary for every Kingdom leader is to be sound in doctrine, understanding the Kingdom. Thus, Paul writes to Timothy and states that we should pay attention to ourselves and the doctrine and continue in them, so that we save ourselves and those who hear us (1 Timothy 4:16). The ambassador is charged with the task of preparing you for your global Kingdom mission.

What is the Diplomatic Mission?

The embassy's diplomatic mission, according to a compilation of scriptures, can be summed up as follows:

1. *Evangelize the unsaved* – We have the authority to bring people to Christ by being a witness (Acts 1:8).
2. *Expose Satan* – It is our responsibility on this foreign soil to expose Satan. We must let people know that Satan is real. At the same time, we have to be spiritual and realize that we do not wrestle against flesh and blood (Acts 26:18, 2 Corinthians 10:3-6).
3. *Expose the sin nature* – Romans 6:23 says that the wages of sin is death and the gift of God is eternal life. Romans 3:23 says that all have sinned and come short of God's glory. It is our responsibility to expose people to their sin nature. People will not naturally wake up one day and say, "I am a sinner."
4. *Expose others to sin* – We exhort and admonish other believers to obey God, making evident violations of spiritual and moral ethics. There are benefits and blessings in obedience (Galatians 5:19).
5. *Expose others to God's love* – People should understand how strong God's love is for them by how we demonstrate love to each other (John 3:16; John 13:34-35, Romans 5:8, 1 John 4).
6. *Entice people into the Kingdom* – There is an old cliché that says you can lead a horse to water, but you cannot make him drink. True, but you can give him a salt tablet and make him thirsty (Matthew 16:17-18).
7. *Educate people about our Kingdom* – We ought to be able to tell people why we believe (1 Peter 3:15, 1 Timothy 4:16).
8. *Engage and establish His presence here on the earth until He comes* (church planting) – The book of Acts gives us the model for Kingdom worship before Christianity as a religion was established: Word multiplied, people being saved multipled, disciples multiplied, churches multiplied (Acts 6:7; 9:31; 12:24).

If what you are doing does not involve these things, you are doing something wrong. You are not living a Kingdom life. You are still living for yourself. Remember, we are not here to make a living; we are here to give life. These above eight areas are the more dominant aspects of the diplomatic mission and are not meant to exclude other aspects, e.g., supporting the Kingdom financially. But I deem these necessary in order to understand how we should fulfill our Kingdom mission. We must act as salt and light to make the King's presence known among people.

Ask yourself these questions: Are you living for the Kingdom or are you living for yourself? How do you know without a shadow of a doubt that you are living for the Kingdom and that your mission in life is now Kingdom oriented?

The Embassy's Theocratic Structure and Culture

"But seek first the Kingdom of God and His righteousness, and all these things shall be added to you." – Matthew 6:33

Then Jesus called a little child to Him, set him in the midst of them, and said, "Assuredly, I say to you, unless you are converted and become as little children, you will by no means enter the kingdom of heaven." – Matthew 18:2-3

But Jesus said, "Let the little children come to Me, and do not forbid them; for of such is the kingdom of heaven." – Matthew 19:14

Seeking the Kingdom should be our number one priority in life, the gas that drives our engine. Unless we become converted, actually changed by the renewal of our minds, and become as little children – totally transparent and trusting – we cannot enter the Kingdom of God. That means our initial focus has to be on the King and His Kingdom; not the church and its traditions.

But how do we practically work this out, living in the Kingdom as Kingdom citizens, but working in and through the church? Remember that the Kingdom of God is here, but not fully manifested, but is definitely a present reality. The greatest and clearest Kingdom manifestation that we know about and have experienced: being born again! This is the greatest mystery above all. The scales fall off of our previously blinded eyes, we are regenerated, and now we can actually see the Kingdom. However, you can be faithful in the church, yet be absent from the roll in the Kingdom of God (Matthew 7:21). We cannot be awed by any other manifestation other than the manifestation of change. The change is in our focus, life mission, and priorities that produce a different lifestyle and culture of living.

> *Jesus answered and said to him, "Most assuredly, I say to you, unless one is born again, he cannot see the kingdom of God." Nicodemus said to Him, "How can a man be born when he is old? Can he enter a second time into his mother's womb and be born?" Jesus answered, "Most assuredly, I say to you, unless one is born of water and the Spirit, he cannot enter the kingdom of God. – John 3:3-5*

A Kingdom citizen changes natures, rulers, and purposes; at salvation, we are "born again". "Unless a man is born again" means in the Greek, *anothen*, "to be born from above". Thus, at salvation, we gain dual citizenship in the country of our natural birth and also in the Kingdom of God, the place of our spiritual birth (Ephesians 2:19). The government of your citizenry ultimately manages your conduct. We belonged to a subordinate, earthy/human kingdom with a destiny based on our sin nature. But through Christ's substitutionary death and our identification with His death, which redeemed us from the power of sin and death, we were reborn from above and regenerated from our sin nature. But regeneration can only occur as one dies. Christ died for your sin nature, so now when you come to Him, it is strictly to die. You must engage in a daily process of dying to your sin nature (Galatians 2:20).

Though we die, we have also been co-resurrected with Him (Colossians 3:1) and now take on His existence – the life He would have lived – and live by faith. My affections are now set on things above (the Kingdom of God) and not on things below (the material, natural world).

Our great salvation involves three aspects: we are saved, we are being saved, and we will be saved. Put in theological terms, every Kingdom citizen experiences salvation, sanctification, and glorification. When we acknowledge who Christ is, what He has provided through His atoning death on the cross, and invited Him to be Lord of our lives, we were saved. This aspect of salvation involved a deep understanding that our present life was an offense to God and was under the sentence over eternal death and hell. This is what positions us to be regenerated, the acknowledgement of our sin nature not simply our sins. A sin nature will always produce sin. Thus, when we allowed Christ to become Lord of our lives, we essentially said we did not want to be Lord of our own life because of our sinful propensities based upon our sinful nature. Then, on the basis of our free moral agency or free choice, we invited the Holy Spirit to awaken our dead spirit. This re-awakening of our spirit man is called regeneration or "being born from above".

Man was made in the image of God, tripartite – spirit, soul, and body, given intelligence to analyze, and was bestowed with authority to tend and keep God's garden. Adam's very existence was worship unto God. However, after Adam, the federal and seminal head of all mankind, disobeyed God, original sin or fallen nature caused all men to be made sinners (Romans 5:12). Adam continued to exist, cursed to work by the sweat of his brow, but his existence was no longer spiritually intimate with God. His spirit died, as promised by God, because he violated the principles of the King and the garden (Genesis 2:17). But it was also promised that one day the Seed (Christ) of the woman would bruise the head of the serpent, Satan (Genesis 3:15).

Christ overturned the power of bondage that put distance between God and man through His death on the cross and His ministry of reconciliation that invited sinners to be reconciled with God (Acts 26:18). This, beloved, is the foundation of the first of the three aspects of salvation, we are saved.

"Being saved" is the process of sanctification – the gradual work of the Spirit transforming the mind of the regenerated believer on a daily basis to the image of God (Romans 8:29). The believer is a dual citizen with dual appetites – appetites for the kingdom of this world and the Kingdom of God. This places man in a sort of internal dualistic battle; however, the spirit man is superior to the flesh or natural man according to the Kingdom principles of subjugation and domination (Romans 6:14, Galatians 5:16-18). So while we are learning to gain the mastery over our sinful or carnal appetites, we are under grace, not under the law. Hence, we are more than a conqueror and no one can bring a charge against God's elect (Romans 8:33). Thus, sanctification is our legal "wiggle" room (justification or acquittal) to engage in the process of change without eternal consequence. Why? Because I'm saved by grace, not by works, lest any man shall boast. You are the predestined work of God already completed in Christ (Ephesians 2:8-10).

"Will be saved" speaks of glorification, which is the process of disrobing the flesh and living totally in the spirit. Glorification is the taking off of mortality and putting on immortality (1 Corinthians 15:35-58). This will happen either at our natural death or the rapture, whichever comes first.

Regeneration is the foundation of seeing and entering the Kingdom and places us in the Kingdom. We commence our new life, our transformational new birth, at the point of death, i.e., when we are crucified with Him. We were instantaneously placed with Jesus to sit together in heavenly places (Ephesians 2:6).

But Christ sent us back into the world with a new nature and new citizenship. We now have a new DNA, and this is how we are able to live in the Kingdom and serve to further the Kingdom's diplomatic mission through the church. Indeed, Christ is clear that just as He is not of this world, neither are we of this world (John 15:19; 17:16). Christ chose us out of the world (John 15:19), and we have died with Him from the basic principles of the world (Colossians 2:20) Paul, in one of many passages, comments on the character, the DNA, of this new man or woman:

> *Therefore, as the elect of God, holy and beloved, put on tender mercies, kindness, humility, meekness, longsuffering; bearing with one another, and forgiving one another, if anyone has a complaint against another; even as Christ forgave you, so you also must do. But above all these things put on love, which is the bond of perfection. – Colossians 3: 12-14*

In a nutshell, as Kingdom persons, we live according to the mandates, edicts, and principles of our King, not the dictates of the world (1 John 2:15). We are submitted to the Kingdom structure and order that He has established for His embassy.

A local church is an embassy and should reflect Christ the King. An "ambassador" is one who is in a five-fold ministry office (2 Corinthians 5:20, Ephesians 4:10-11). If you are not in the five-fold ministry, you are not an ambassador. Everyone that serves under an ambassador is a minister. The ambassador must fulfill the sovereign's will – he or she acts on direct authority from the King, Jesus. As the person directly over all foreign affairs, ambassadors:

- Are placed in a specific place to prevent war, i.e., the church holds off the anti-Christ
- Advances the cause and culture of the Kingdom
- Engages in the economic development of the citizenry
- Assists citizens in protecting against "terrorism" from Satan by exposing his schemes

- Protects citizens against "drugs", i.e., the seductive and intoxicating philosophies of the world which set themselves against the knowledge of God.

The ambassador represents the King, while ministers represent the Kingdom government and are dispatched to spread the order of the Kingdom. When Paul states that we are ambassadors (2 Corinthians 5:20), it is clear that he is referencing the apostolic and not the general laity or ministers of Christ. He implores the laity to be reconciled to God on Christ behalf or as Christ's representative. If you are unclear about the issue of the embassy, an embassy is where ambassadors are sent to serve. The United States (US) has embassies across the world representing US interests and spreading US principles and philosophies for living. Embassies are simply where ambassadors serve and operate on behalf of its sending country. The ministers function under the ambassador and assist in executing the will of the sending kingdom or country.

The duties of ministers serve the overarching purpose of fulfilling the Great Commission in Matthew 28:19. They should:

- Serve as a royal priesthood and act as intercessors on behalf of the Kingdom (1 Peter 2:9)
- Serve as ministers of reconciliation (2 Corinthians 5:18)
- Serve as light and salt in the world (Matthew 5:13-14)
- Serve as fishers of men (Mark 1:17)
- Serve as a living epistle to those in our life space (2 Corinthians 3:3)
- Witness (Acts 1:8)

The Kingdom citizen has direct orders to impact the context in which they have been assigned through an embassy (church) that has been given the keys or access to the Kingdom. Wherever the embassy exists, the Kingdom is present!

Hence, Kingdom citizens carry diplomatic immunity – no weapon formed against you shall prosper! You are the property and responsibility of the King and His Kingdom. You do not have to worry about opposition; just stay close to the embassy and make sure that you are connected to the soil of the embassy. The embassy is the pick up place if domestic chaos occurs or conflicts. In the event that a war or terroristic events begin to take place in the country where the embassy is, the sponsoring country will send air transportation to gather its citizens and take them to safety from the embassy. This is why in the natural, all US citizens are advised to check into the embassy when they go to a foreign country. If conflict and chaos breaks out, the embassy can contact you, come get you, and bring you to safety. The Bible states that there will be a conflict and chaos of immeasurable proportion that will take place beginning with the emergence of the anti-Christ, who despises our King, and will launch attacks against His citizens and those who admire their principles. The scripture states that before this takes place (tribulation), that Christ will come and rescue or retrieve the citizens of His Kingdom through the embassy or church (1 Thessalonians 4:16-18). Thus, the Bible clearly states that Christ is coming back for the church, not the individual (Ephesians 5:27).

To really understand the purpose of the church, one must really understand the concept of an embassy. To understand the concept and role of an embassy, you must understand the role and purpose of an ambassador (Ephesians 6:20, 2 Corinthians 5:20). To understand the role and purpose of the ambassador, you must understand the concept of discipleship and Kingdom expansion through the calling and sending of ambassadors (Romans 10:14-17, Ephesians 4:11, Jeremiah 3:15, Acts 9:15-16). Every Kingdom citizen is tasked with the responsibility of exposing foreigners to the Kingdom with the message of the King – a heralder of the King's message! The embassy is the branch of the Kingdom that is responsible for expanding the King's influences globally (Matthew 28:19-20).

So what is the church? Jesus asked His disciples, "Who do men say that I am? And Peter answered, "You are the Christ, the Son of the living God." Then Jesus said to Peter that flesh and blood did not reveal this to him, but His Father in heaven and upon this rock He will build His church (Matthew 16:13-18). The word "church", or *ekklesia*, means those that have been called out, invited, or summoned for the service of the Kingdom. It is a political term that denotes the gathering of a cabinet. When we refer to the church, we are referring to a gathering of a cabinet of representatives.

The church is literally to function as an embassy. It should be a reflection of Christ's Kingdom on the earth. The Greek word for "kingdom" is *basileia* which means "sovereignty, rule, realm, royalty". So when you step into the Kingdom, you are moving into the realm of God's power. The Kingdom is when God is ruling and reigning with His authority in your life. Our responsibility is to represent Him and His interests, not our own. As you prioritize His needs and desires, then He promises that all other things will be added to you. Christ said the church should be concerned or consumed with this: the keys to the Kingdom (Matthew 16:19). This means that the church is the custodian of the Kingdom. The work and the role of the church is to usher people into the Kingdom of God. And if you, as a member of a church, are not ushering people into the Kingdom of God, you cannot claim to be a part of the church Christ defined!

The church's role is to bring people into the Kingdom. However, one of the major problems hindering the church's role is that people in the church have not come into the Kingdom themselves. It is hard to bring people into something that you have not walked in yourself! Jesus never said you must be born into the church – He said you must be born again. He taught that your regeneration is the sole pathway to seeing and entering the Kingdom. When we are born again, we should get a visual of the Kingdom that is so clear that we are able to step into the Kingdom.

But some, perhaps most, have stepped into the church, and we have built a social construct that is void of God's spiritual Kingdom. Without this backing from God, we cannot access the power of the King and, rather than being transformed by the renewing of our mind, we are being conformed to the image of the world in which we exist.

The church's conformity to the world is evident, and this is one of the reasons why the message of the Kingdom of God has been lost in the church. More and more, the church has taken on the organizational characteristics of the world around it, democratic rather theocratic, and created and followed its own 'traditions' that are not grounded in the Word of God or the Kingdom of God. Why is that so important? It is so important because the Bible teaches us that there will come a time when Jesus will not be in the church (Revelation 2 and 3). In the gospel of Matthew, Matthew refers to the Kingdom of God as the Kingdom of heaven, but for Matthew, the terms are synonymous as previously mentioned. Most people think the Kingdom of God means going to heaven, but it has both an eschatological (futuristic) manifestation and an existential (right now) manifestation. Thus, the church is ignorant of the Kingdom of God and its mandates today. Jesus said He ushered in the Kingdom and that the Kingdom of God was in our midst.

A real sign of the Kingdom is power and not just a word. The Kingdom comes with the demonstration of power. Jesus went preaching the Kingdom of God, teaching the Kingdom of God, and healing every disease that was among them. Our church traditions include preaching and singing, but overall, no one is being delivered and set free. The devil is putting us to sleep inside the church and Matthew 7:21-22 records Jesus saying:

"Not everyone who says to Me, 'Lord, Lord,' shall enter the kingdom of heaven, but he who does the will of My Father in heaven. Many will say to Me in that day, 'Lord, Lord, have we not prophesied in Your name, cast out demons in Your name, and done many wonders in Your name?' And then I will declare to them, 'I never knew you; depart from Me, you who practice lawlessness!'

These are church people that attend every Sunday, believing they are doing the Lord's work. Be they never entered the Kingdom! In the above verse, those who cry "Lord, Lord" discover that Christ never knew them and that they were not allowed entry into the Kingdom. If they were doing all of these things in Jesus' name, how could Jesus say they were practicing lawlessness?

The central message of the Kingdom of God is "Go and make disciples" – evangelism and discipleship. "By their fruits, you will know them", said Jesus in Matthew 7:20. The bottom line is fruit; what fruit are you bearing for the Kingdom? The clearest fruit you can bear is making disciples. That is the harvest.

You cannot replace the gospel of the Kingdom with the gospel of altruism and humanitarian efforts. You must know and encourage others to know the King. Jesus followed the rabbinic tradition in His ministry wherein He proclaimed, explained, and demonstrated the Kingdom. So the expansion of the Kingdom is practiced with proclamation, explanation, and demonstration. And demonstration equals power! And the greatest demonstration of power is when the unbeliever believes in the King – at that point, they have entered the Kingdom and are placed under the instructions of an ambassador and an embassy.

Kingdom Expansion and Culture of Invitation

As representatives of the Kingdom, stationed in embassies (churches) across the globe, we all have one goal in mind: we expand the Kingdom of God on earth by fulfilling the Great Commission.

The day and time where the church appealed to our society and served as the source of truth for most communities is gone. There was a period of time where people went looking for churches, however; according to the most recent research people are no longer attending churches like they used to. Kingdom citizens must become knowledgeable and wise when expanding the Kingdom.

What kind of character and personality does the Kingdom citizen, as described in Matthew 5:1-11, 13-15, have? Not taking into account personality differences, every Kingdom citizen must stand out as being sincere in living what they believe, whose good works point people to their Father, the King, and whose character/personality draw people to Christ. In Matthew, Jesus uses two elements to describe the general role of Kingdom citizens: salt and light. Firstly, the Kingdom citizens should realize that they are a change agent: salt brings flavor to that which was bland and preserves something from rotting, and light illumines darkness.

Salt awakens flavor, but it also preserves; and it is something which causes men to thirst for living water. According to God everything is dark until light appears. Light speaks of illumination, revelation, truth, transparency, knowledge, purity, and is the source of life. Stott observes, "The basic truth which lies behind these metaphors and is common to them both is that the church and the world are distinct communities...The world is evidently a dark place, with little or no light of its own...The world also manifests a constant tendency to deteriorate." So a Kingdom citizen should bring understanding by shining light on the darkness in people's lives.

Where should Kingdom citizens be salt and light? In our places of influence: jobs, professional and social organizations, frequent places we visit, etc. People on your jobs should want to know how you perform so well and how you maintain your composure under stress and loss. By doing the opposite of what a person who does not know God does, men see our good works and glorify our God in heaven. Salt can lose its saltiness; light can give way to darkness. Similarly, Christians can lose their influence and purpose in the world. And yet, they and only they can make a transforming difference in the world. As salt is of value only when it is used and light only when it shines, so Christians are of value only as they serve their purpose in the world. Failure to do so renders them irrelevant. A Christ-like life blesses us, expresses itself in redemptive service to others, and glorifies God.

Organizational culture is extremely important in creating an environment of invitation. Every organization or system of people that gather for a particular purpose on a consistent basis has what is called organizational culture. Ministry culture – the values, assumptions, and beliefs shared by members of a particular organization and taught to new members as correct, will be the deciding factor of whether or not a ministry is able to create an environment that supports its ministry goals.

What Does Research Suggest?
George Hunter suggests that in the West we are living in a new apostolic era, and America is a wide open mission field. There are at least 120 million functionally undiscipled people in America 14 years and older. America is a secular nation, not "one nation under God." Other countries are now sending missionaries to our country to win people to Christ. Many have said, "Had it not been for the initial efforts of western missionaries, we would not have a relationship with Christ today".

Thus, many nations feel, not only the conviction of the Great Commission and the Spirit of God, but a sense of obligation due to America's mission work of the past. But today, believe it or not, America is one of the new mission fields, and this qualifies us as existing in a new apostolic era.

What are the characteristics of an apostolic era? For the first three centuries of Christianity, the Christian movement had to achieve four objectives according Hunter:

1. They faced a population with no knowledge of the gospel; the Christian movement had to inform people about the life, teachings, and ministry of Christ; they had to explain to people the gospel of the Kingdom, its claims, and its offers.
2. They faced hostile populations and the persecution of the state – the church had to "win people and influence people" in order to persuade people to have a positive attitude about the movement.
3. They faced an empire with several entrenched religions; people had to be convinced of the plausibility of Christianity.
4. They had to invite people to Christ and become apart of the Messianic community and follow the life and teachings of Christ.

The early church had to be very intentional about these objectives in order to win people to Christ. Christianity did not exist in a favorable environment, and in order for the Christians to be effective in their Kingdom mission, they had to create a culture that was receptive to Kingdom expansion. Reading these characteristics, do they sound familiar? They should – these are the characteristics of this day and age and like the 1st century church, Kingdom citizens must become intentional about making the expansion of the Kingdom our culture and way of life.

Research suggests that the number one reason people don't attend church is because they are not invited (Thomas Rainer, *The Unchurched Next Door*). Christ stated in Matthew 9:37-38 that the harvest is plentiful but the laborers are few. There are thousands of people that desire to know Christ, but Christians do not invite them to church or dialogue about Christ. The following are the top ten surprises about the unchurched and how they feel about church:

1. Most unchurched people prefer to attend church services on Sunday mornings if they attend.
2. Females are likely to be the most antagonistic or the most receptive to the gospel.
3. Most of the unchurched feel guilty about not attending church.
4. Eighty-two percent of the unchurched are at least likely to attend church if invited. Christians are not inviting the unchurched to church. Only 21% of active church members invite anyone to church in the course of a year, but only 2% of those invited are unchurched.
5. Very few of the unchurched have had someone share with them how to become a Christian, and Christians have not been very influential in their lives.
6. Most of the unchurched have a positive attitude about pastors, ministers, and the church.
7. Some types of cold calling are effective and others are not.
8. The unchurched would like to develop a real and sincere relationship with a Christian.
9. The attitudes of the unchurched are not correlative to where they live, their ethnic or racial background or their gender. They are not a monolithic group. The only pattern that research revealed a correlation was concerning income. The higher the individual's income, the more resistant to the gospel he or she is likely to be. Jesus told us that it would be difficult for people with money to enter the Kingdom of God (Matthew 19:24) .
10. Many of the unchurched are more concerned about the spiritual well-being of their children than themselves.

In order to reach the harvest, we must create a culture of invitation for Kingdom expansion within the embassy and in the lives of all Kingdom citizens.

The Necessity of Creating a Culture of Invitation for Kingdom Expansion

Without a culture of invitation, an embassy will experience minimum growth and ministry exposure. When we speak of invitation, it can be as simple as simply asking someone to attend church or as involved as developing a relationship with an unbeliever to influence them toward a relationship with Christ. Many pastors are disappointed Sunday after Sunday due to the lack of church attendance. Members themselves can become judgmental about their own church and ask the question, "Where are the people?" However, empty seats simply mean that the embassy has not created a culture of invitation for Kingdom expansion. This is normally due to the lack of personal invitation. Jesus emphasized the Kingdom expansion model in the parable of the man who gave a great supper (Luke 14:16-24). In this model, he invited guests and when they would not come, he told his servants to bring the poor, maimed, lame, and blind. Then he told them to go into the highways and hedges and compel people to come to his supper. Kingdom citizens must invite, bring, and compel people to enter the Kingdom of God. Our King has a friendly, welcoming and highly inviting Kingdom that accepts everyone that responds to His invitation.

In today's social climate, as a rule of thumb people are not going to just show up to your church. Would you expect someone to just show up and knock on your door and ask can they eat with you without being invited? Church, for a lot of people is a very intimate place that is designed for specific people that have a family atmosphere – a place where people can feel intrusive if they are not invited.

As a result, people see churches as family groups bonded around a common knowledge and purpose so they tend to feel like outsiders and don't feel comfortable inviting themselves. If you don't invite people, don't expect them to come; and if you invite people, plan for them to come.

Chapter Four:
The Kingdom and the Seven Churches of Asia Minor
(Revelation Chapters 1-3)

The message of the Kingdom was clearly the message of the early church and the early church was definitely a mission-driven church. So the question that must be echoing in your mind is – what happened to the contemporary church? How did things get so out of control? Through one of His dearest disciples and apostles, John, Christ left us a strategic map that would help navigate us prophetically through the entire church age. This strategic map is located in the first three chapters of the book of Revelation embedded in the seven churches of Asia Minor.

The seven churches of Asia Minor allow us to gain greater insights to the culmination of the Kingdom. These seven churches represent the entire existence of the church or the church age. The church is dispensational, which means it was not present in the Old Testament and will not be present when the events of Revelation chapters 4-21 unfold.

The Importance of Preaching the Kingdom of God

Why is preaching the Kingdom of God so significant now? Jesus Christ's intention of the church was to preach the Kingdom (Matthew 16:16-19). Eschatologically, the church age comes to an end once the message of the Kingdom is preached throughout the world: "And this gospel of the Kingdom will be preached in all the world as a witness to all the nations, and then the end will come" (Matthew 24:14). Eschatologically, Jesus is knocking on the doors of the Laodicean church, the 7th church of Asia Minor, seeking to be heard by anyone who can hear Him, in a church age that considers itself to be rich in increase, lacking nothing, while not knowing that they are blind, wretched, miserable, poor, blind, and naked (Revelation 3:17). They are neither cold nor hot in their works. By the way, if you are unfamiliar with the term "eschatology" it means "the study of the end times or the end".

The Contemporary Church

The contemporary church has lost its divine mission. It is not the church that Christ built. Its mission has become self-centered according to Revelation 2 and 3 and is based upon:

- Financial prosperity
- Independence

Instead of existing for the purpose for which it was intended (Matthew 28:19-20), the church has become weak, impotent, anemic, sightless, and suffers from diplopia. Many churches today do not know or teach biblical truth or sound doctrine. Many of our contemporary churches begin with rebellion or submission issues and birth churches that focus on carnal interests, further compromising the Kingdom agenda for the sake of their issues.

Simply ask yourself these questions:

1. Do you prefer to be part of a church with people like you in race, class, or gender because you feel uncomfortable around diversity?
2. Do you pray to fulfill God's wishes on earth or for God to fulfill your wishes on earth?
3. Do you pray for someone other than yourself and have you seen your prayers answered?
4. Do you have compassion for the lost and invite them into the Kingdom of God? Do you invite them to your local church? Or, do you believe that one's faith is a personal decision that everyone should respect?
5. What is the Kingdom and what does it have to do with you?
6. Is your life consumed with your career, your family, and your friends or is it consumed with making disciples?
7. Do you consider scriptures mandating "making disciples" and "not considering what you have as your own" as outdated or unrealistic?

8. Are you magnetic, energetic and enthusiastic about the Kingdom of God, learning more in order to teach or impact someone else with the message of the Kingdom?
9. Are you focused on sanctification struggles or making disciples?
10. Are you able to give a defense for what you believe according to scripture?

When you consider these questions, how do you think your 'Christian' friends would answer them? Let's examine the seven churches in light of these questions!

The Road to the Laodicean Church

According to the scriptures in Revelation 2 and 3, the church age is coming to a close and will be followed by the rapture, as noted in Revelation 4. Revelation 4 begins with John being caught up into heaven, which is interpreted by many evangelicals including myself, as a picture of the great snatching away referred to as the rapture. The word "rapture" does not appear in the scriptures, instead the phrase "caught up" in 1 Thessalonians 4:17 means "snatched up" in the clouds to meet Him. After the rapture, chapter 4 of Revelation begins a series of events called the seven year Tribulation or Daniel's 70th week. The Tribulation will be the most macabre time in human history. The anti-Christ will be on the rampage for seven years and ultimately lead an attack against Israel. You and I should not be here during this period, if we are living as Kingdom citizens on a Kingdom mission. An invitation to participate in the rapture, however, will be extended to those who were able to overcome the Laodicean church age, the most dominant church in the end times (Revelation 3:21). Those who overcome the Laodicean church age are those who are able to hear the voice of Jesus Christ, answer His call, and embrace His way of life by carrying His vision, culture, keys, and authority to spread the message of the Kingdom of God throughout the world.

How did we move from a mission-oriented church to a self-consumed church? There is an existential (here and now) and dispensational (over time) explanation for where we are in the prophetic time clock of God. As Kingdom citizens, we need to be able to discern the times and seasons of God and make sure that we are prepared to meet Jesus, as well as, encourage others to meet the King. Christ gives us insight to the start and finish of the church age in the book of Revelation. However, before we delve into the church age, you must understand how God partitions time.

Dispensationalism

God has done and will do unique things at specific times, to give a unique marking so that we can know where we are on His prophetic clock.

Time from the creation of man to the creation of a new heaven and earth has been divided into seven unequal periods or dispensations (Ephesians 2:7; 3:2). These periods are marked off in scripture by some change in God's method of dealing with the sin and responsibility of man. Each of the dispensations ends in judgment, marking man's utter failure in every dispensation. Five of these dispensations, or periods of time, have been fulfilled; we are currently in transition from the sixth dispensation into the seventh dispensation. The sixth dispensation culminates with the end of the church age and the rapture. The final dispensation is the culmination of human history as pictured in Revelation chapters 4-22.

You and I must have the spiritual ability to discern the times (Ephesians 5:15-17, Romans 13:11). We need to have the spirit of discernment like the sons of Issachar; we must discern times and seasons to know where we are in the prophetic time clock of God. According to Ecclesiastes 3, there is a time and season for everything under the sun.

Everything in life is governed by times and seasons and must run its course; even our lives are in God's hands (Psalm 31:15).

People, revelation, events, evolution, understanding, and the world are governed by dispensations or times and seasons. Divine providence and omniscience suggest that God is in control and is bringing all things together (Romans 8:28). Everything is headed in one specific direction, to one climactic closure. This is referred to as dispensationalism.

While supercessionists believe that the Jews' only opportunity to accept Christ is prior to the rapture, just like that of the Gentiles, dispensationalists believe that God has a unique plan for those Jews who do not accept Christ in time for the rapture, in light of God's covenant with Abraham. Also, God's prophecy of the 70 weeks in which He deals with the sin and transgression of Israel stopped right before the 70th week at the death, burial, and resurrection of Jesus Christ. It is believed by many scholars that each week represents seven years, because Christ was crucified 483 years since this prophecy was given to Daniel (Daniel 9:20-27). This leaves one more week of years to be fulfilled, which would equal 490 years or 70 weeks of years. The final week is believed to be the Tribulation period, after the rapture of Christ's church. God's continued favor is on the Jews even after the church age. While God engrafted us into the covenant, He still has a special purpose for Israel. The following chart shows how God deals with man over time, dispensationally, and how we, the church, have related to God dispensationally.

Seven Dispensations of Theology Proper: God's Ways of Working With Man Within Certain Timeframes
1. Dispensation of Innocence – from creation to the fall of Adam. Man failed in this dispensation by eating of the tree of knowledge (Genesis 2:16-17; 3:22-24). **Judgment** – cast out of Eden
2. Dispensation of Man's Conscience from the Fall of Adam to Noah (the flood) – Man failed in this dispensation by choosing to do evil over doing good (Genesis 6:11-13). **Judgment** – the flood
3. Dispensation of Government from Noah to the Tower of Babel/ Abram – Man was called to be fruitful and multiply; however, they were doing this void of God (Genesis 9:1, 11:1-8). **Judgment** – confused their tongues at the Tower of Babel
4. Dispensation of Patriarchal Rule from Abram to Moses – Age in which God establishes the Abrahamic covenant, promising Abram that he would be a great nation (Genesis 12:1). **Judgment** – Israelites violated the conditions of the covenant (faithfulness and obedience) and entered into Egyptian bondage
5. Dispensation of the Law from Moses to Christ – Israelites repeatedly violated the laws established. **Judgment** – exile and diaspora to this current day
6. Dispensation of Grace from Christ to the Rapture – Church age granted unmerited favor due to the sacrificial death, burial, and resurrection of the Lord Jesus Christ. This church age is immersed in an unbelieving world and an apostate church – the church of Laodicea. **Judgment** – Rapture of God's invisible church, leaving others to remain for the Tribulation period
7. Dispensation of the Millennial Reign of Jesus Christ – Christ reigns with His saints for 1000 years and Satan is bound (Revelation 20:1-6). Satan is then released for a little while and gathers an army against Christ, but fails. **Judgment** – Great White Throne of Judgment

Judgment surely is coming as it had come for previous dispensations. We exist in the 6th dispensation.

We need to ask – what can we learn from those who have lived before us to ensure that we personally do not face a judgment that separates us from God's eternal love and protection? In the current 6th Dispensation of Grace (Theology Proper), man has sought to understand who God is and what man's responsibility is in relationship with God. I developed the following chart as a result of an analysis of the church and its theology from a comprehensive and historical perspective. This chart will assist you in understanding the current status of the church and how God will bring the message of the Kingdom of God at this time. I coined this chart the Seven Dispensations of Theological Renewal. This chart will help you understand the movement of theological thought and biblical understanding through the ages.

Seven Dispensations of Theological Renewal
(New Testament)
Man's Understanding of Their Role and Responsibility towards God

1. Dispensation of Revelation *(1st-3rd centuries)*
What does the Kingdom mean?

- The early church was given the most comprehensive understanding of the gospel of the Kingdom and the mission of Christ; the early church represented the most powerful representation of the call and cause of Christ that we know.
- The early church was the first and only dispensation in which the mind of God was understood concerning His Kingdom, the church, and the world.
- Thus, the gospels and the book of Acts serve as a historical record of the intended focus and scope of the mission of the church and its teachings. This era is called the Dispensation of Revelation, because during this time, the Holy Spirit inspired holy men to write the Word of God.
- The early church was persecuted for its faith, dispersed, and its leaders became martyrs for the faith; its impact lasted until Christian persecution ended.

2. Dispensation of Identification *(312 AD - 16th century)*
Who is Christ?

- This dispensation was birthed in the 4th century upon the cessation of Christian persecution with the signing of the Edict of Milan. This official document ended Christian persecution and allowed Christians to freely practice their faith.
- This period is known as the Roman Catholic era. Persecution ended when the church 'married' Constantine the Great and became the state religion. Roman religious practices were merged with Christianity. To be a Roman citizen was to be a Christian and to be a Christian was to be a Roman citizen; you no longer had to have an experience with God or be born again to be a Christian.
- This era opened doors of the church, allowing the faith to experience the peace and tranquility the church, collect of all the writings of the apostles, and decide on the official doctrine and practices of the church.
- Four major councils that helped us to identify who God is by defining our Christology, pneumatology, and 'trinitology', etc.: Council of Nicaea (325 AD), Constantinople (381 AD), Ephesus (431 AD), and Chalcedon (451 AD).
- The Dispensation of Identification allowed the church to fully identify who Christ was in relationship to God the Father and God the Holy Spirit. During this era, Christ was declared, *homousia*, or of the same substance as God and serves as the origin of our present-day understanding of Christ as both Lord and Savior and God.
- After careful study of the scriptures, Christ was declared fully God and fully man, while not confounding or mixing the two natures of Christ. This is the dispensation wherein we identified who God was in relationship to His triune presentation – One God in Three Persons. Many of the most renowned theological thinkers, commonly referred to as the patristics or early church fathers, emerged from these councils. Many of them, originating from Northern Africa, became known for developing the primary doctrines of the church formally named church creeds.
- Some of the most important creeds that came out of these councils were: the Nicene Creed, the Constantinople Creed, the Athanasian Creed, and the Apostle's Creed.

3. Dispensation of Salvation *(1450s - 1600s)*
What does it mean to be saved?

- During this period, the theology of the Roman Catholic Church was beginning to be challenged by men such as John Wycliffe and John Huss.
- This period is known as the Reformation period; the Reformation period culminated under the efforts of Martin Luther who had an experience that caused him to re-examine the scriptures concerning what the church taught about eternal life and how one obtains eternal life (soteriology).
- Luther challenged Roman Catholic scholars to an open theological debate concerning salvation by nailing his 95 theses or statements against the theology of the Roman Catholic Church on the door of the church in Wittenberg. Luther's research led him to conclude that salvation cannot be granted by the Roman Catholic Church or through penance or prayers for the dead.
- He coined four Latin phrases: *sola fide, sola gratia, sola scriptura, sola Christos* – "by faith alone, by grace alone, by scripture alone and by Christ alone is one saved"; outside of those things, we are not saved.
- Luther was not attempting to shut the doors of the Roman Catholic Church; he was simply challenging the church to rethink its teaching.
- Luther was not a lone ranger in this endeavor; men such as John Calvin and Ulrich Zwingli also challenged Roman Catholicism and its lack of biblical basis for its beliefs and practices.
- As a result, the Reformation movement gave birth to Protestantism – in all its denominational forms.
- This is the Dispensation of Salvation, because Luther's treatises serve as the basis for our soteriology or doctrine of salvation today.

4. Dispensation of Regeneration *(1700s - 1830s)*
"You must be born again!"

- This dispensation has its roots in the English Reformation. Known as the Revivalist Period, and the Great Awakening, during this time, men of God emphasized you must be born again; you must have an experience [Jonathan Edwards, George Whitefield, John and Charles Wesley, D.L. Moody, Charles Spurgeon, etc. in England, Scotland, and America].
- John and Charles Wesley, George Whitefield, and others were also instrumental in influencing religious groups, like the Quakers and the Puritans, toward religious pietism. Their message focused upon regeneration; they were instrumental in re-instituting the message of regeneration in the church for two centuries.
- Wesley focused upon ensuring that people had the internal witness of the Spirit of God to confirm that they were a child of God. Wesley stressed the spiritual experience; he saw the need for believers to have two encounters with God, salvation and perfect love, because both were acts of grace.
- This is the Dispensation of Regeneration, because the message of conversion was preached and embraced in the 18th and 19th century.
- In America, the Great Awakening period produced the message of rejuvenation and gave birth to the first black Baptist church in mid-18th century America – Silver Bluff Baptist Church of Aiken County, South Carolina.

5. Dispensation of Impartation
"Be filled with the Holy Spirit" *(1830s - present)*

- This dispensation gave birth to the re-visitation of the Holy Spirit to unify and empower God's people for service after Pentecost. While this dispensation probably represents one of the most controversial dispensations within the Protestant movement, this is the dispensation of the Spirit-filled experience, evidenced by glossolalic speech, or "tongues".
- Early in the 20th century, God sent an over-abundance of His Spirit to a group of people worshiping on Azusa St. in California.

- The Azusa experience was typified by an expansive and spectacular baptism of the Holy Spirit, glossolaic speech, miracles, and other gifts of the Holy Spirit manifested.
- The Holy Spirit ignited His people for ministry, but to no avail. Racism in America and the lack of sound biblical doctrine minimized the movement in America. Racism and hatred were too prominent for whites to identify with blacks, even in church.
- Social and racial battles ended the initial movement; Pentecostalism was disdained, and society deemed the entire movement heretical primarily because God chose a one-eyed black man named William J. Seymour to popularize the movement.
- Seymour received the teaching for this experience from a white gentleman by the name of William Parham. Historians suggest that Parham, who was a KKK sympathizer, never experienced glossolalic speech. However, the Holy Spirit was first believed to have fallen upon one of Parham's students, Agnes Ozman.
- Despite opposition, the Spirit-filled experience, known as the Pentecostal movement in the 1900s, spread around the world.
- This movement took place during a time when one of the most heretical, theological works (although heralded as one of the most scholarly works of that time) was published: *The Negro: A Beast or in the Image of God* by Professor C. Carroll. His work was labeled a scientific and theological project that would educate Americans about the place of negros in America. He stated that blacks (pre-Adamites) belonged to the animal kingdom of beasts and were created on the fifth day.
- Unfortunately, the Pentecostal movement did not unite God's people, but further divided them along the lines of race and class and began to be identified with the rigidity of the holiness movement and the classism of the Assemblies of God.
- This movement continues today as the most vital and vibrant aspect of the Body of Christ, crossing denominational lines, racial lines, and geographical lines.

6. Dispensation of Participation *(1950s - present)*
"Have you received the Holy Ghost since you believed?"

- This era covers what has been called the Pentecostal/ Charismatic/Full Gospel movements. The 6th dispensation of theological renewal was the dispensation wherein man was now an active participant in worship and engaging their faith.

- Word of faith, praise movement, charismatic, full gospel, neo-Pentecostalism, intercessory prayer, and spiritual warfare were birthed during this time. This movement gave birth to prayer ministries, such as "Can ye not tarry for one hour?" by Dr. Larry Lea.

- This dispensation is also responsible for the praise and worship movement that created a new genre of interactive music, praise dancing, and the integration of the fine arts in worship.

- The 6th dispensation was the era in which men were allowed to express their faith and the formality of religion was subtly abandoned. The need for formally trained clergy diminished and an emphasis on Bible training was traded for experience.

- Laymen no longer demanded that their leaders be trained in the Word, and denominations who demanded trained leaders declined, so this dispensation has produced a generation of ignorant pulpits: men and women, who taught simply from inspiration, totally void of information through education.

- Thus, this dysfunctional charismatic movement reflects the culture in which we live, rather than the culture of Christ.

- Out of this movement, health/wealth/prosperity teachers emerged – a natural progression from a church divided along racial and class lines. This era is the greatest foundation for the Laodicean church.

7. Dispensation of Exaltation *(1980s - present)*

"The gospel of the Kingdom of God must be preached and then the end will come"

- This is the Dispensation of the Kingdom of God. Jesus' primary message, heralded by John the Baptist, and disseminated through the disciples and the 1st century church was the Kingdom of God (heaven). Now God is raising up preachers teaching the Kingdom, preparing people for the end of the church age and the beginning of Christ's rule in heaven during the Tribulation period, then on earth for 1000 years. Then, time ends for all mankind, and we step into eternity.

- This era re-emphasizes the Messiahship of Christ or Christ as King sitting on a throne. Christ's presence upon the earth, while redemptive in nature, was royal in reality, He is King!

- This era also prioritizes the Kingdom mandate: Christ came to make Kingdom citizens through regeneration and discipleship.

- From the 4th century to the 21st century, believers were finally challenged to focus upon the proclamation, explanation, and demonstration of the Kingdom of God – the things Christ focused upon when He was here.

- This is the dispensation wherein truly Spirit-filled people will abandon the banner of traditionalism and church, which is rooted in the sociological whims of a racist, classist, and heretical church.

- Becoming a Kingdom citizen, who is no longer under the primary rule of the 'king of this world', requires that you understand what you came out of and how your life operated before salvation, what you have accepted as your new life in Christ's Kingdom, and how your spiritual life should be governed from now on. This will lead to a reprioritization of everything formally associated with your existence – now that you are repurposed.

- Christ has a set aside a people, the remnant, who will come out from among those who have a form of godliness, but deny the power – the Church of Laodicea.
- This remnant are the overcomers, who despite its unpopularity, have distanced themselves from people who have learned to enjoy church without Christ for so long that they no longer have the ability to recognize that He is no longer present in the building as King.

Do You See the Pattern?

Putting the charts side by side, we can get a clearer picture of what God has done thorough the ages that is bringing the church to the Kingdom message. The trends we see are not happenstance, but the times and seasons of God.

Dispensations (Theology Proper)	Common Theme	Dispensations of Theological Renewal (New Testament)
Innocence – creation of man, walked in the presence of God	Purest relationship with God	*Inspiration/ Revelation* – birth of the church at the Day of Pentecost
Conscience – Adam to Noah	Who is God?	*Identification*
Government	Faith alone, not indulgences, dictates a relationship with God	*Salvation*
Patriarchal Rule – Abrahamic covenant	You must have an experience that connects you to the covenant of Abraham	*Regeneration* – You must be born again

Dispensations (Theology Proper)	Common Theme	Dispensations of Theological Renewal (New Testament)
Law	We must fulfill the commands of our King – law showed us we could not do it in our power; Impartation of the Holy Spirit empowers us to do His work	*Impartation*
Grace	Granted grace to participate in the work	*Participation*
Millennial Reign	The end of time	*Exaltation* (Kingdom)

Do you see where you are in the prophetic time clock of God? Do you see a consistent pattern in which God is working with man? God gives His prophets some insight into what He will do with His people – and they have all come to pass. An example in prophecy that shows dispensationalism at work is in Ezekiel 36,37,38 – God promised the prophet that after the diaspora (dispersion of Jews to all four corners of earth) that miraculously He would bring them together to be their own state/nation. This occurred in 1948. Enemies surround Israel; however, they are unable to overcome Israel – "not by might nor by power, but by my spirit says the Lord"...!

We know the prophecy concerning the gospel of the Kingdom is coming to pass because until now, very few pulpits had been teaching the Kingdom of God – it was not the dominant message of the church. Now we are at a turning point, because the message that I feel a burning to declare will, prophetically and eschatologically, usher in the coming of the Lord.

It is the message of the Kingdom that creates the expectation of the return of the King. Many churches today do not want the Lord to come; they want the Lord to give them total dominion over the acquisition of material wealth. However, He is not coming back until the message of the Kingdom is preached; hence, we are now headed toward our last reformation of the church. This brings us to understanding the history of the church in order to see where we are in a spiritual sense.

The Churches of Asia Minor

We are approaching the end of the 6th dispensation of grace (Theology Proper) in the church age. However, the church age includes seven churches of Asia Minor described in the book of Revelation, each of which have existential (here and now significance for their times) and eschatological (end time) significance. In biblical numerology, the number seven (7) represents the number of completion. The 7th church represents the last church disposition of the church age and will be the context in which the rapture will take place.

First Church of Asia Minor – Church of Ephesus
The Apostolic Church, Era of 30 AD to 100 AD, Revelation 2:1-7

This was the Apostolic church, the church in the house and the temple, the Kingdom-driven church, and church of revelation.

- **Commendation** – This church had a discerning spirit and they labored for Christ's namesake (Revelation 2:2).
- **Condemnation** – They left their first love. Participants in this church were commanded to repent and do the work of ministry. The early church became busy doing the work to such a magnitude and forgot the King. Doing Kingdom work without emphasizing the King is unacceptable.

Second Church of Asia Minor – Church of Smyrna
The Persecuted Church, Era of 100 AD to 312 AD, Revelation 2:8-11

This was the greatest time in church history of persecution of the church of Christ. During this time, Satan tried to obliterate the church due to the effectiveness of the apostolic church preaching the Kingdom. Over 5 million Christians were killed for trying to preach the gospel.

- **Commendation** – This church was under persecution and did not have much of anything. To be a Christian was degrading. Many were not allowed to live an open productive life and were killed for being a Christian: burned at the stake, rolled down mountains in spiked barrels, burned on torches, wrapped in animal skins, fed to wild animals, simply because of their faith.
- **Condemnation** – Not a word

Third Church of Asia Minor – Church of Pergamos
The Indulged/Compromised Church, Era of 312 AD to 606 AD, Revelation 2:12-17

This city worshiped many Greek idols and was known to be Satan's capital city since the decline of Babylon. It is the place where the Edict of Milan or Toleration was signed, creating the Christian religion under Constantine the Great. This was a covenant made by ordained clergy with pagans. The doors of the church officially opened in this era, not by God, but by a man with a political agenda – Constantine the Great!

- **Commendation** – They held His name and did not deny the faith even amidst persecution, mostly because they came in on the tail end of persecution. Part of this church went through persecution. The historical aspect of what this church represents is compromise.
- **Condemnation** – This church was married to the world rather than to Christ. Christ rebuked the church for fraternizing with those who held the doctrines of Balaam and the Nicolaitans.

Fourth Church of Asia Minor – Church of Thyatira
The Pagan church, 606 AD to Tribulation, Revelation 2:18-29

Characteristics we see in this church are still around. Where some things had a stopping point, others continue on through the tribulation.

- **Commendation** – Christ has six specific commendations for Thyatira: deeds or works, love, faith, service or ministry, perseverance or patience, and "deeds of late are greater than the first."
- **Condemnation** – During this era, forms, rituals, and ancient mystical practices were introduced into Christianity. Acts and symbols of worship to pagan deities were increasingly incorporated into the church's practices.

Fifth Church of Asia Minor – The Church of Sardis
The Dead Church, 1520 to Tribulation, Revelation 3:1-6

This is the church of the Reformation, the "escaping ones" or "those who come out". Even the church of the Reformation, the Lutheran church, became a state church of Germany, which caused them to be authorized without being born again.

- **Commendation** – Seeking to break from the heretical teachings and practices of the Roman Catholic Church, reformers, such as Martin Luther and John Calvin, emerged.
- **Condemnation** – The reform began by Luther and Calvin did not launch the church into widespread radical change – even though the Protestant church was created. Reformationists were still connected to dead stuff! As a result, God referred to Sardis – the would-be reform church – as the dead church; it promised much, but in the end, delivered little.

Sixth Church of Asia Minor – The Church of Philadelphia

The Church Christ loved, Born Again Church, 1750 to the Rapture, Revelation 3:7-13

Church of Philadelphia was a missionary church, a Great Awakening church, preaching the message "be born again" throughout the world. This church will make known those who say they are Israel, but are not, and are of the synagogue of Satan. Christ is the One who holds the key, opening and shutting the door that no one can open or shut. Therefore, this era is about opening and shutting doors. It is the remnant church that exists amidst the dominant church.

- **Commendation** – Christ commends this church for keeping His Word, not denying His name, and persevering. For those actions, Christ promises to keep them from the tribulation.
- **Condemnation** – Not a word, this is the only church that will not go through the tribulation. Everyone else does! Only two churches had no condemnation – Philadelphia and Smyrna.

Seventh Church of Asia Minor – The Church of Laodicea

The Lukewarm Church, 1900s to present, Revelation 3:14-22

The 7th church of Asia minor, Laodicea, says that it is rich in increase and has need for nothing – a money-driven church, with money-driven preachers, and money-driven members. People who serve money, whether in the pew or the pulpit. People are at the crossroads of evangelism or economics, choosing whether to serve the god of mammon or fulfill the mission of the King. This church is indifferent, irresponsible, and illiterate about the King and their responsibility to Him, having become intoxicated with self-promotion and self-preservation. Hence, they have fallen away from doctrine, Christian duty, discipleship, and discipline. Instead, they look for popularity, personal fulfillment, and a minimal price tag when considering church membership.

- **Commendation** – Not a word
- **Condemnation** – Lukewarm, wretched, miserable, poor, blind, and naked, and do not realize it. Christ advised the Christians of this city to buy from Him "white garments" of purity and righteousness. Jesus appealed to them to buy salve from Him for better spiritual vision. He appeals to those in this church to come out and sup with Him.

This is the church age we live in, the final church age of the 6th dispensation.

In biblical numerology, the number 6 is the number of man. It was on the 6th day that God made man and then on the 7th day, He rested from His work. During the 6th dispensation of theological renewal, the number of man, what happened between the time of the 6th Church of Philadelphia, which received no condemnation to the 7th Church of Laodicea that received no commendation?

Satan methodically removed the message of the Kingdom and replaced it with the message of the church and made it a social institution, rather that a spiritual organism. People allowed culture, class, race, unbiblical traditions, etc., to rule over the authority of Christ's culture and the role of His holy nation. If we look at the North American church, we can see how the church of Laodicea was born:

Freedom Church
Protestants became tired of classism and battles between Protestantism and Catholicism, and came to America for religious freedom. But they used oppression and de-possession of Native Indians' land for their freedom.

Slave Church

Slaves were needed to develop the land at the pace that the English wanted, so they needed slaves to build their new world.

Though Africans were also in America as indentured servants and freeman, the colonists instituted slavery as the means to build their new world. Thus, Indians were placed in restricted areas called reservations, and blacks were declared slaves, a little higher than animals and forced into slavery. Eventually, they used Christianity to codify it. The Society of the Promulgation of Gospel in Foreign Parts wanted to make the slaves Christians. The slave owners said no, prohibiting slaves from being baptized, ensuring they are not equal to whites. They resolved this by declaring that blacks were 3/5th human.

Reconstruction Church (1865)

Church of racial hostility in the name of God. The South heralded the practices of Jim Crow (separate but unequal). This was a period of time when slavery ended in the law books, but not in the culture and the mind. Thus, this period concretized the separation of the races in churches. Blacks were not allowed to worship with whites, and whites would rather die than to be caught worshiping with blacks. It was well understood that there was nothing to be gained in the black church. The black church was simply the haven for blacks to release their expressions of pain through singing, dancing, clapping and shouting in their churches. The black church was considered illiterate and spiritually insignificant by the dominant race and that mentality still exists today in the 21st century.

Spirit-filled Church (1906)

The church that was supposed to bring it all together with the coming of the Spirit on Azusa street, was the Spirit-filled church, which emerged in a segregated society. The coming of the Spirit as at Pentecost was to reverse the curse of racism and segregation. For a moment, it appeared as though it might, because God used a one-eyed black man by the name of William J. Seymour to make it popular. Unfortunately, the weeds of division and segregation based upon racial superiority took over the movement.

While the Church of God in Christ became the official Pentecostal Church that all Pentecostal ministers white, black, etc., had to come to be ordained, another movement of Pentecostal separatist whites met in Hot Springs, Arkansas and created the Assemblies of God. So if the Spirit of God erased the color line, the majority led church drew it again.

War Church

During this time, the church was a refuge for the community, emerging as vital part of America. The post-World War II church gained a significant position in American society due to the casualties of war and their impact upon the family and the society at large. So the church was the place were people attended and became the place of social influence for politics, race, class, and gender. This movement also created a strong movement that used the church as political vassals to execute its Democratic or Republican agendas, which further divided the church along the lines of race, class, and political parties.

Civil Rights Church

This church instituted the social programming of the church. The Civil Rights church, while historically playing a very vital if not the main role in the liberation of the oppressive practices of the American people and politics against blacks, had become spiritually impotent. Most of the churches that once engaged in justice ministries forgot all about God's Kingdom due to the protest against the kingdoms of this world. We are supposed to use our US citizen's rights and power of the vote to cast our political desires. However, the Civil Rights church, in my humble opinion, did not understand times and seasons, thus when the assignment was executed, it kept pushing the social agenda at the expense of ignoring the spiritual agenda. Please understand – this is not the posture of all African-American led churches nor does it represent the majority today, but there still remains a significant number of churches that push the civil rights agenda and not the Kingdom of God. This has left us with social movements with no spirituality.

Segregated Church

The denominational churches developed branches for minority congregations that maintain the separate but equal philosophy. Everyone knows that this was not a valid practice nor principle, but it assists the human conscience on paper.

Classist Church

You can come if you represent success! This church was the church of the upper class; if you were someone of importance and with wealth, you were welcome into this kind of congregation. These congregations existed within every ethnic group and was a place for what they considered their 'elite' people. Of course, this is not a Kingdom principle or practice, which further supports the argument of the socialization of the church.

Laodicean Church

This is the church of prosperity, of those who are now trying to get paid. This church is the health, wealth, prosperity, and dominion theology church. It is the church that believes its mission is financial independence and a mansion now! This church evaluates its success by the amount of material gain that is accumulated, not by the number of disciples made. This church tends to be benevolent, but not evangelistic; it is easier to give out of your abundance to the poor than it is to make disciples. The Bible states that the poor will be with you always and what profits a man to gain the world and lose his soul. The Bible does not suggest that everyone remain in poverty, because that is not a Kingdom principle either, but the fulfillment of the Great Commission is the commandment of God. The church must be about the Father's business (John 4:34; 9:4).

95

As we close the 6th dispensation, we must remember the foundation that was built for Christianity during this period of time:

- Discernment
- Commission-oriented, not state-driven, churches of risk; their mission could and did cost them their lives
- Had to contend with synagogue of Satan – counterfeit Christians, saying they were Christian, but were not (Revelation 2:9; 3:9)
- Disciples – each church was told, "to him who overcomes", which means in every era, someone got out with Christ
- Doctrine – during the Roman Catholic Church era, we were allowed to stabilize our doctrinal beliefs:
    1. Christology, Council of Nicaea, 324-532 AD – understanding of Christ
    2. Pneumatology, Council of Constantinople, 381 AD
    3. The Bible (Old and New Testament) was codified, Council of Carthage, 397 AD
    4. Patristic teachings, doctrinal teachings from Athanasius, the Three Cappadocians, Augustine, Ambrose, Chrisostum, Jerome, etc.
    5. Trinity, from Basil of Caesarea, Gregoria of Nicaea, Gregory of Nazianzus
    6. Christology, Council of Ephesus, 431 AD
    7. Two natures of Christ, divine and human, Council of Chalcedon, 451 AD
    8. Despair out of the church – monasteries
    9. Disgrace out of the church – crusades for Christianity – raped, killed, murdered, and stole in the name of the Lord
    10. Disgrace of slavery in Christianity
    11. Disgrace of exploitation of Africa in the name of God and the pope – 1431
    12. Disgrace of witchhunts against women wanting to be used by God – First message of Christ was given to women – "tell disciples I've risen"
    13. Disconnect out of the church – taught people how to be Christians without intimacy – priest, the Bible

Dispensations are about times and seasons, and ultimately it is about disciples. Let's review for a moment. By the time of the 1700s to the early 20th century, the only thing that we, as the church, regained and recaptured from the early 1st church was: who God is, how one is saved, and in order to be saved, you must be born again, and how one is empowered for service. Almost 2000 years later, that was the remnants of the Kingdom message. As you can see, one of the reasons the church is crippled and its members are ignorant and trapped inside is because we need theological renewal. We left the doctrine of the early church and have been poisoned through the opened doors of the church that have allowed everything in and out!

Christ is looking for true and sincere worshipers – disciples, not Christians. We want to identify with the church of Philadelphia, not Laodicea, standing in line behind the King as He knocks on the door of the Laodicean church. We should not want to get into what He has been locked out of. Jesus said His mission was to teach the Kingdom of God. Thus, our mission is to embrace, understand, and teach the Kingdom of God, because it is our eschatological assignment. We are a privileged, prophetic, chosen people amidst many who do not hear the message of the Kingdom, because they are too busy having good church!

Chapter Five:
The Kingdom and the King

The Kingdom Message From a Biblical Perspective

Now that we have looked at my analysis of where the Kingdom message began and where it is today, it is important to look at the Kingdom from a biblical perspective. A quick review of the synoptic gospels will reveal that the Kingdom was spoken of by Christ frequently. As followers of Christ, we must pay particular attention to any teaching He repeatedly emphasized. So, we must ask ourselves "Why is the message of the Kingdom of God important?" "Does it have existential significance?"

These questions are answered somewhat when you consider the voices which proclaimed the Kingdom's coming and culture. The only message recorded as being preached by John the Baptist in the wilderness was that of "Repent for the Kingdom of God/heaven is at hand". The inaugural message of Christ's ministry, as recorded in Matthew 4:17, was "Repent for the Kingdom of heaven is at hand". Additionally, the parables taught by Christ as recorded in Matthew 13, Mark 4, and Luke 8 were preached in order to introduce and familiarize the masses with the nature, character, and structure of the Kingdom. Also, in Acts 1:3, we see Jesus teaching the disciples things concerning the Kingdom of God, and in Acts 28:31, we see Paul, preaching and teaching the Kingdom of God. If John the Baptist, Jesus, and the Apostle Paul were concerned about the Kingdom of God, its importance should be obvious. However, the true importance of these teachings is revealed by Christ when he states:

> *"And this gospel of the kingdom will be preached in all the world as a witness to all the nations and then the end will come". – Matthew 24:14*

The end time message is the message of the Kingdom of God! It is the message that will usher in the coming of the Lord, Jesus Christ.

Defining the Kingdom of God

The Kingdom of God was the message John the Baptist preached, it was the message Jesus preached, and it was the message of the New Testament 1st century church. As followers of Christ, we must learn the message of the Kingdom of God and learn what is required to gain entrance to His Kingdom. To fail to do so puts one in danger of living out Matthew 7:21-23 which says:

> *"Not everyone who says to Me "Lord, Lord" shall enter into the kingdom of heaven, but he who does the will of My Father in heaven. Many will say to Me in that day, 'Lord, Lord, have we not prophesied in Your name, cast out demons in Your name, and done many wonders in Your name?' And then I will declare to them, 'I never knew you; depart from Me you who practice lawlessness!'*

Christ states that when He returns, there will be people on the earth who performed miracles, cast out demons, and prophesied – all in His name, but were never known by God! Christ never knew these individuals intimately. Why? Because they failed to enter the Kingdom! These individuals will doubtless spend eternity separated from the King they never knew. This conclusion naturally causes one to ask the questions – what is the Kingdom, where is the Kingdom, and how does one enter the Kingdom?

What is the Kingdom?
In John 18:36, Jesus states "My Kingdom is not of this world...my Kingdom is from another place" (NIV). In another passage, Jesus states "The Kingdom of God is near/among you" (Luke 10:9). What did Christ mean by this statement? In this text, the Pharisees are consumed with Jesus showing them the Kingdom. They had been waiting for the coming Messiah who had been prophesied to come to overturn evil and restore Israel to power. Jesus told them that the Kingdom of God is among you. The word "among" is translated as *eggizó* in the Greek, which means "come near; approach".

In essence, Jesus was telling the Pharisees that His Kingdom was all around them, but they were incapable of seeing it because they sought to see it with their natural eyes. According to Acts 4:24, God is a spirit. The word "kingdom" refers to the domain or territory under the sovereign rule of a king. Thus, the phrase "Kingdom of God" is the spiritual realm of God's authority where His culture governs its citizens. The Pharisees were expecting a natural political kingdom to come in with much pomp and circumstance. Jesus let them know that His Kingdom was a spiritual kingdom.

> ...*righteousness and peace and joy in the Holy Ghost...*" – *Romans 14:17*

In Romans 14:17, the Apostle Paul states that the Kingdom of God is not meat and drink (concerned with natural thing or things pertaining to the flesh), but is righteousness, peace, and joy in the Holy Ghost. What does this mean?

Righteousness
In 2 Corinthians 5:21, scripture says:

> *For He made Him who knew no sin to be sin for us, that we might become the righteousness of God in Him.*

"Righteousness" is the Greek word *dikaiosune*, which means "right standing". In Hebrew, righteousness is translated as *tsedek*, which means "to be right with God". Romans chapter 3 tells us that Jesus is our righteousness. According to Isaiah 64:6, because of the Adamic sin nature, the righteousness of man is comparable to that of a filthy rag – a rag used to clean the afterbirth of a woman who has just delivered. In the Old Testament, when a person committed a sin, he was required to face the penalty of death. However, God created a system of grace and atonement, through the sacrifice of burnt offerings, which allowed the blood of animals to restore fellowship between the offender and God.

Depending upon the magnitude of the sin committed, an animal of a particular size and type, free of blemishes and defects, was sacrificed on behalf of the sinning individual.

The sacrificial animal was taken to the priest who would then present it to God in the form of an offering. Just before it was slain, the man would lay his hand on the head of the perfect (sinless) offered animal – thereby transferring the perfect condition of the offering to the offender and the sins of the offender to the sinless offering. The offender was declared righteous, and the offered animal died a substitutionary death on behalf of the sinner.

> *And he brought the bull for the sin offering. Then Aaron and his sons laid their hands on the head of the bull for the sin offering. – Leviticus 8:14*

The shed blood of this perfect offering would satisfy the requirement set forth by God as payment for the penalty of the sin committed. When John the Baptist saw Jesus, he said, "Behold the Lamb of God who comes to take away the sins of the world." Because Christ lived a perfect and sinless life, He was the only acceptable sacrifice that could pay the penalty for the sins of all mankind. He took our sin and gave us His righteousness that we might have fellowship with God the Father. Thus, we cannot get into the Kingdom based upon our own righteousness. Every time we think we deserve to be saved, we are not experiencing the Kingdom. Our righteousness is not achieved; it's imputed and has been declared by Christ. Thus, we have been declared righteous!

Peace

Righteousness precedes peace. According to Romans 5:1, because of the blood of Jesus Christ, we now have peace with God the Father. Peace (*eirene* in the Greek) means "inner rest, harmony, free from anxiety", and it is translated from the Hebrew word *shalom*, which means "completeness, soundness, welfare".

Sin separated us from God. Christ put on sin and gave us His robe of righteousness. Thus, in accordance with Colossians 3:3-4, we enjoy invisibility with the Father "...for your life is hidden with Christ in God. When Christ who is our life appears, then you also will appear with Him in glory." When the Father looks at us, He sees us through the prism of Christ's righteousness, which means God is never 'mad' at us. You cannot violate Him, and you have peace with Him as long as you stay inside Christ's righteousness. Once we have peace with the Father, then we can enjoy peace with one another.

Joy in the Holy Ghost

If having been declared righteous and at peace with God the Father, there is no reason not to have joy. Joy (or *chara* in the Greek) is an internal disposition of appreciation, satisfaction, gladness, or inner happiness, which originates as a result of my relationship with God. According to Paul, the Kingdom is about being in the spirit of God, which serves as the promise, guarantee, or deposit of God, which assures your place in God's eschatological Kingdom when it comes in its fulfillment.

Jesus – The King of the Kingdom

What is the Difference Between a King and a President?

In government, the president is an elected officer who serves as head of state and sometimes as chief executive. In countries where the president is chief of the state, but not of government, the role is largely ceremonial with few or no political powers. Presidents may be elected directly or indirectly for a limited or unlimited number of terms.

Throughout biblical history, nations have desired for someone to lead them in their national (political, military and financial) affairs. In short, these nations desired a king. Ideally, the king was the wisest and most powerful person in the nation and had to have demonstrated the ability to lead a nation to triumph.

The king was intelligent and a warrior who could prevail over the enemy and outside pressure.

Through its kings, Israel established an empire that stretched from Mesopotamia to Egypt and was allowed to take her place among the other nations in the fertile crescent and enjoy economic boom and political fortune. Israel's monarchy was established by Saul, David and Solomon.

> *In those days there was no king in Israel; everyone did what was right in his own eyes. – Judges 17:6*

> *Then all the elders of Israel gathered together and came to Samuel at Ramah, and said to him, "Look, you are old, and your sons do not walk in your ways. Now make us a king to judge us like all the nations." – 1 Samuel 8:4-5*

The office of king was so important to the Jews, there are two books called 1 and 2 Kings, which record all the kings of Israel's history and the prophets who prophesied to them. These books cover Israel's history until the northern kingdom or division of Israel, comprised of ten and a half of the tribes, is sent into Assyrian captivity in 722 BC and the southern division or kingdom is sent into Babylonian captivity in 586 BC. Through all of this, God allowed Israel to understand that their kings were inefficient and did not have the ability, character, and power to lead them to ultimate triumph. God was trying to remove the desire and taste for human leadership from Israel's mouth, so they would allow Him to become their King.

> *And the LORD said to Samuel, "Heed the voice of the people in all that they say to you; for they have not rejected you, but they have rejected Me, that I should not reign over them. – 1 Samuel 8:7*

The Bible says blessed is the nation whose God is their Lord. A king and leader can decide the spiritual tone of their nation.

The kings and queens of England fought to establish the religious practices of that nation – Catholicism vs. Protestantism. While human kings are fickle and limited, there is a King who is all-wise and compassionate, truly sovereign, omnipotent, omniscient, and omnipresent. The psalter asked the question many have been unable to answer in Psalm 24:7-10 – who is the King of Glory? The New Testament answers this question clearly. His name is Jesus. He is the one true King!

He is the one who ascended to the throne of David and His Kingdom shall have no end (Isaiah 9). Christ's Kingdom does not highlight political dominance and economic muscle, but is characterized by righteousness, peace, and joy in the Holy Ghost according to Romans 14:17. He is greater than any king that has ever lived, has triumphed over every other kingdom that has ever existed, and will ultimately triumph over the world as described in the book of Revelation, which ends with Christ reigning as King!

Characteristics of Christ the King

1. He is a seated king.

> "In the year King Uzziah died, I saw the Lord sitting on a throne, high and lifted up, and the train of his robe filled the temple. – Isaiah 6:1

A throne is a chair of state of a high dignitary or sovereign. A king seated on his throne can do whatever he wants to do. Christ as King is unlimited in power and potential. He has complete sovereignty over people, resources, and all created things in the world. His throne is characterized as being high and lifted up. So in order to see the King, you have to do what the psalter said, "Lift up your head oh you gates". We are the gates and if He is going to come in, we have to lift up our heads, because He is high and lifted up.

The fact that Christ is seated indicates that He has rested from His labor. Genesis states that on the seventh day, God rested from His labor and saw that all He had created was good.

Colossians 3:1 states that Christ is seated at the right hand of God the Father. The posture of sitting indicates that everything that will be done has already been completed by God. Jesus Christ was slain before the foundation of the world. Thus, God has already walked through your life, and you are simply awaiting a manifestation of what has already been.

2. His throne is characterized as strong and mighty.

> *"Who is this King of glory? The Lord strong and mighty, the Lord mighty in battle. Who is this King of glory? The LORD of hosts, He is the King of glory. – Psalm 24: 8, 10*

Christ is not impotent and unable to change things on our behalf. He has all power and can set anyone free and turn any situation around. Referring to Colossians 3:1 again, this scripture also indicates Christ's strength and authority. In the Old Testament, the Hebrew word for "hand" is *yad* and is symbolic of one's might, power, and ability. Thus, statements in scripture such as, "...the Lord upholds him with his hand" (Psalm 37:24) and "no one can snatch them out of my hand" (John 1:28) refers to much more than God's dexterity. Also, the right hand is considered to be the stronger of the two hands. Thus, Christ being seated at the right hand of God indicates that He is in the greatest seat of power and authority imaginable!

3. His throne is characterized as gracious and helpful.

> *Let us therefore come boldly to the throne of grace, that we may obtain mercy and find grace to help in the time of need. – Hebrews 4:16*

We do not have a dictatorial and non-compassionate King. He can sympathize with our infirmities and knows what it means to suffer. Christ was incarnated, not voted into His position. He has walked in our shoes and knows what it means to be tempted and tried as we are. Therefore, when He is in state and you ask Him "Have mercy on me!", He can be merciful.

4. His throne is characterized by freedom and judgment.

> For we must all appear before the judgment seat of Christ, that each one may receive the things done in the body, according to what he has done, whether good or bad. – 2 Corinthians 5:10

> Then I saw a great white throne and Him who sat on it, from whose face the earth and the heaven fled away. And there was found no place for them. – Revelation 20:11

In 2 Corinthians 5, Christ is seated at the judgment seat of believers, and in Revelation 20, He is at the Great White Throne of Judgment. At the former, He frees believers to live in eternity and, at the latter, He sentences people from the everlasting presence of God into a future of pain and suffering in the lake of fire.

5. He is a supernatural King.

> Then He arose and rebuked the wind, and said to the sea, "Peace, be still!" And the wind ceased and there was a great calm. But He said to them, "Why are you so fearful? How is it that you have no faith?" And they feared exceedingly, and said to one another, "Who can this be, that even the wind and the sea obey Him!" – Mark 4:39-41

Christ came into the world through sinful flesh. Because of His lineage as a child of God, He was not from the bloodline of Adam and was therefore perfect. Christ took upon Himself, through Mary, human flesh in order to walk among us.

He divested and veiled himself of His divinity, so that He could relate to you and me and eventually save us from our sins. Christ came consumed with humanity. So when we talk about our King, He was fully God and took on human flesh. Thus, Christ was fully God, and fully man.

6. He is a serving King.

> "...just as the Son of Man did not come to be served, but to serve, and to give His life a ransom for man." – Matthew 20:28

The Kingdom of God is characterized by service. Christ came to serve and repeatedly demonstrated for the disciples that the greatest in the Kingdom are those that serve.

Access to the King and the Kingdom

So how do you gain entrance to the Kingdom of God? The church has the exclusive right and possession of the keys of the Kingdom of God. No one can get to the Kingdom without the church. Because revelation gets you into the Kingdom, no one will enter unless we allow them access by sharing the revelation of Jesus Christ as Lord.

Everyone is familiar with the concept of "joining the church" but admittance to the Kingdom is not secured as easily as walking to the front of the church and giving your hand to the preacher. When we talk about entering the Kingdom, we talk about entering into the reign of God. When you give your life to Christ you die, go to heaven, and are sent back to serve as a representative of the King. This is the new birth Christ spoke of in John 3:3, which says:

> Jesus answered and said to him, "Most assuredly, I say to you, unless one is born again, he cannot see the kingdom of God."

Therefore, you must be born again to even see the Kingdom of God.

How do you know when you have seen the Kingdom of God? Jesus answered this question when he responded to John the Baptist's inquiry regarding whether He was the Messiah. Jesus responds by saying:

> *The blind see and the lame walk; the lepers are cleansed and the deaf hear; the dead are raised up and the poor have the gospel preached to them. – Matthew 11:5-6*

Thus, we see or experience the Kingdom of God when the effects of original sin are overturned in someone's life. The message of the Kingdom of God is always accompanied by signs and wonders as evidenced by the following scriptures:

> *And Jesus went about all Galilee, teaching in their synagogues, preaching the gospel of the kingdom, and healing all kinds of sickness and all kinds of disease among the people. – Matthew 4:23.*

> *Then Jesus went about all the cities and villages, teaching in their synagogues, preaching the gospel of the kingdom, and healing every sickness and every disease among the people. – Matthew 9:35*

The Kingdom of God is always accompanied by a demonstration of power. Jesus went preaching the Kingdom of God, teaching the Kingdom of God, and healing every disease that was among them. Ephesians 2:6 says that we have been made to sit together with Him in heavenly places. So when you gave your life to Christ, you were then, immediately, seated with Him. When He sent you back, you became a minister of foreign affairs, and your life was no longer your own. We live to serve the King. In order to enter the Kingdom, scripture tells us that we must become as a little child and fulfill the will of God for our lives.

> *Not everyone who says to Me, 'Lord, Lord,' shall enter the Kingdom of heaven, but he who does the will of My Father in heaven – Matthew 7:21*

...and said, "Assuredly, I say to you, unless you are converted and become as little children, you will by no means enter the kingdom of heaven – Matthew 18:3

As such, you must no longer operate based upon the habits, characteristics and tendencies you received through your natural genes. Instead, you are called to humble yourself as a child and allow the Holy Spirit to teach and mentor you into acting out of your newly received Kingdom DNA – the fruit of the Spirit.

But the fruit of the Spirit is love, joy, peace, longsuffering, kindness, goodness, faithfulness, gentleness, self-control. – Galatians 5:22-23a

The word "fruit" is singular, not plural. Thus, it is impossible to have "mastered" or "manifested" one of these characteristics and be lacking in others. The manifestation of the fruit of the Spirit is a result of a transformation of your DNA as you walk in the Spirit (Galatians 5:16) – not the process of gradual sanctification.

Love	Universal, spiritual love, overwhelming compassion and understanding; affection without criticism or limitation.
Joy	Internal disposition of gladness based upon an expected outcome despite experiential circumstances. A strong feeling of great happiness, delight, a state or source of contentment or satisfaction.
Peace	Wholeness of life; right relationship or harmony between two parties or people, often established by a covenant; a state of mental or physical tranquility; calm, serenity.
Longsuffering	Opposed to shortness of mind or soul, irascibility, impatience, intolerance; fortitude, patience.

Kindness	Compassion, sympathy, benevolence, consideration and helpfulness.
Goodness	Goodness involves not only right behavior but also avoiding its opposite, evil.
Faithfulness	Full of faith, trustful, and not simply trustworthy.
Gentleness	Sensitivity of disposition and kindness of behavior, founded on strength and prompted by love; excellence in character or demeanor.
Self-Control	Moderation, restraint.

The Kingdom citizen must be willing to sacrifice the life that was lived prior to seeing the Kingdom, in order to gain admission to the Kingdom. The great sacrifice that is required to enter God's Kingdom is demonstrated in the Parable of the Pearl of Great Price in Matthew 13:45-46. The merchant, who discovered the "great pearl", sold all that he had in order to obtain this treasure of immeasurable value. That, too, must be our attitude if we desire to enter the Kingdom of God.

Our Response to Christ the King

What then should be our response to the King once we enter His Kingdom? Isaiah 6:1-10 provides a paradigm of what our life in the Kingdom should resemble.

In the year that King Uzziah died, I saw the Lord sitting on a throne, high and lifted up, and the train of His robe filled the temple. Above it stood seraphim; each one had six wings: with two he covered his face, with two he covered his feet, and with two he flew. And one cried to another and said: " Holy, holy, holy is the LORD of hosts; the whole earth is full of His glory!" And the posts of the door were shaken by the voice of him who cried out, and the house was filled with smoke. So I said: "Woe is me, for I am undone! Because I am a man of unclean lips, and I dwell in the midst of a people of unclean lips; for my eyes have seen the King, the LORD of hosts."

Then one of the seraphim flew to me, having in his hand a live coal which he had taken with the tongs from the altar. And he touched my mouth with it, and said: "Behold, this has touched your lips; your iniquity is taken away, and your sin purged." Also I heard the voice of the Lord, saying: "Whom shall I send, and who will go for Us?" Then I said, "Here am I! Send me." – Isaiah 6:1-8

Reverence (Isaiah 6:2)

Reverence is the attitude one takes toward someone who is deserving of high honor and respect and is usually used to refer to royalty. The angels flew with two wings covering their faces in reverence to the King. By covering their eyes, they were giving honor to God and acknowledging that they were inferior and in the presence of a superior.

Humility (Isaiah 6:2)

Humility is the result of a reverential attitude. Scripture indicates that while in the presence of God, the angels also covered their feet with two wings. The feet represent mobility and direction. The angels' response to the King's presence indicated that they were willing to surrender their own direction and movement and subject themselves to His will. In the same respect, we must give up control of our lives – our direction – and subject it to the guidance of the Holy Spirit. We must "humble" ourselves to the King of kings and acknowledge that He is our Lord.

Service (Isaiah 6:2)

With two wings, the angels flew, which represents service. Isaiah confessed that he was a man of unclean lips and that he lived among a people of unclean lips. Yet, in response to God's call for service, Isaiah said in verse 8, "Here am I! Send me". Once we see the Kingdom, humble ourselves and enter in, our posture and attitude in relation to the King should be service.

Is your life characterized by reverence, humility, and service?

Chapter Six:
The Kingdom Economy

Every kingdom or country has a ministry of finance, treasury, etc. The only way a country or a kingdom can be sustained is to have a business model that generates the necessary resources to support the efforts and activities of the kingdom. Most kingdoms and countries alike refer to this as the tax. In the US., we have an entire branch of government that is responsible for the fiscal affairs of taxation called the Internal Revenue Service in addition to the US Treasury Department and the Federal Reserve; all of these agencies manage the fiscal or financial affairs of our country.

Economics is an extremely important issue, and the ability of a country to generate enough revenue flowing through its country is a decidedly important factor in the power of that particular country. Terms, like GDP (gross domestic product) and GNP (gross national product), are critical to the economic climate of a country. The ability of a country to create jobs through creating an atmosphere for big business and entrepreneurship to emerge is vital to the economy. Businesses create jobs and jobs create tax paying citizens that contribute to the sustainability of the country. Strong economies must have the ability to attract foreign investors and create strong export and import relationships with other countries. Issues, such as interest rates, are critical as it relates to attracting investors. Without going into the world of finance and economics, you get the point that economics is important to any country, and every strong country must have a strong business model for generating the country's resource.

The Kingdom business model is that everything belongs to the King. The earth is the Lord's and the fullness thereof, cattle on a thousand hills belong to Him; all silver and gold belongs to Him, and all souls belong to Him. Thus, the Kingdom model of economics is based upon the King issuing you resources, and you making an increase on what He has given you and bringing Him a high rate of return. Thus, the Kingdom model of economics is a model of stewardship.

Kingdom economics is primarily concerned with three areas: the sustainability of the embassy, the personal welfare of its citizens, and the care for those who cannot care for themselves. Kingdom economics is a part of God's plan to ensure that His church is sustained and its mission executed. It is also concerned with its ministers and their ability to sustain their lives in abundance. When I speak of abundance, I'm speaking of God giving you more than enough. The Kingdom citizen should not be living from paycheck to paycheck; this is not the will of God for citizens who are stationed in strong and emerging economies.

God providing the Kingdom with more than enough, however, also involves the appetites and disciplines of the Kingdom citizen. The Kingdom-wise Kingdom citizen is not deceived by the alluring power of debt. The wise Kingdom steward does not purchase beyond his or her ability to pay a debt back without causing financial stress in other areas. Wise Kingdom citizens are financially disciplined and good stewards over the resources of God.

Our discussion of Kingdom economics will teach us that God requires you to be a good steward of your treasure. This not only translates to being a faithful tither, one who gives ten percent of their gross income, but also to what you do with everything that God has given you – your time, talent, as well as, your treasure. You will also learn about God's holistic system of economics and prosperity. As a Christian, if you do not prioritize God's Kingdom first, you will never truly have prosperity.

As we study Kingdom economics, it is important to note that the laws of Kingdom economics will not work without application of the following laws:

- *Law of Faith* – But he who doubts is condemned if he eats, because he does not eat from faith; for whatever is not from faith is sin (Romans 14:23).

But without faith it is impossible to please Him, for he who comes to God must believe that He is, and that He is a rewarder of those who diligently seek Him (Hebrews 11:6).

- *Law of Sacrifice* – "Most assuredly, I say to you, unless a grain of wheat falls into the ground and dies, it remains alone; but if it dies, it produces much grain. He who loves his life will lose it, and he who hates his life in this world will keep it for eternal life" (John 12:24-25).

- *Law of Obedience* – If you are willing and obedient, you shall eat the good of the land;(Isaiah 1:19)

- *Law of Free Will* – "Speak to the children of Israel, that they bring Me an offering. From everyone who gives it willingly with his heart you shall take My offering" (Exodus 25:2).

- *Law of the Spoken Word* – Death and life are in the power of the tongue, and those who love it will eat its fruit (Proverbs 18:21).

These five laws are the laws that govern the mind of a wise steward of God, in addition to his resources, faith, sacrifice, obedience, free will, and the tongue. The wise steward must trust the King at His Word, if he is to release His resources by faith. The wise steward must understand how to sacrifice, not indulge in everything they can indulge in – learn how to do without. The wise steward must learn to obey the Kingdom principles of God, not simply participate in the activities of God. Kingdom stewards understand that every day they are faced with choices that only they can make, so they must choose the right things. Lastly, the wise steward understands the power of the tongue and watches what they say and disciplines their tongue.

Steward is a word I have used quite often in this chapter, but what is a steward? Let's examine this concept.

Owner – Church vs. Steward – Kingdom

God is the King, and the King owns everything. This premise represents the great divide between Kingdom citizens and church folks. Church folks desire to control their own finances, life, and direction. They have a strong investment in the concept of individual ownership of property and self, because they have been acculturated in a republic that is based on private ownership rights. In the Kingdom of God, any and all resources that you accumulate should be available for use in the Kingdom. Further, God will one day hold us accountable for everything He has placed in our hands.

To understand stewardship, you first have to understand the servant/master relationship. A steward is a manager of the affairs of the master with the best interest of the master in mind, because the steward knows that his master will return and settle all accounts for which he is responsible. The steward understands that the master will then punish or reward based on the steward's stewardship. If you take away the servant/master relationship from the idea of stewardship, then you take away obedience and put sovereignty in the hands of the steward. This is where Adam fell short.

Now the serpent was more cunning than any beast of the field which the LORD God had made. And he said to the woman, "Has God indeed said, 'You shall not eat of every tree of the garden'?" And the woman said to the serpent, "We may eat the fruit of the trees of the garden; but of the fruit of the tree which is in the midst of the garden, God has said, 'You shall not eat it, nor shall you touch it, lest you die.'" Then the serpent said to the woman, "You will not surely die. For God knows that in the day you eat of it your eyes will be opened, and you will be like God, knowing good and evil". So when the woman saw that the tree was good for food, that it was pleasant to the eyes, and a tree desirable to make one wise, she took of its fruit and ate. She also gave to her husband with her, and he ate. Then the eyes of both of them were opened, and they knew that they were naked; and they sewed fig leaves together and made themselves coverings. – Genesis 3:1-7

Adam and Eve had a relationship with God; therefore a relationship with God does not exempt you from the influences of Satan in the area of stewardship. Satan wants to attack us in the area of accountability for what God has given us by distorting the servant/master aspect of stewardship. The tree was only a temptation when Satan entered their thoughts, and just as he did with Adam and Eve, he wants to get you to ignore God and act like you are sovereign. The enemy wants you to manage the treasures in your life as if they belong to you, with your benefit in mind as opposed being a steward over the Lord's goods.

> *For every beast of the forest is Mine, and the cattle on a thousand hills. I know all the birds of the mountains, and the wild beasts of the field are Mine. If I were hungry, I would not tell you; for the world is Mine, and all its fullness. – Psalm 50:10-12*

Lessons of Stewardship

Stewardship and Your Perspective – Being a good steward is impossible to do unless you have the proper perspective about the things in your life. Good stewards learn to take the perspective of their master or king. They learn to see the possessions in their life as God sees them. The key is this: to come into Christ's Kingdom, you must die. Jesus stated repeatedly that being His disciple required the sacrifice of all your rights and possessions, even one's life. In Mark 8:34, Jesus informed us that there is no salvation without a crucifixion: "When He had called the people to Himself, with His disciples also, He said to them, "Whoever desires to come after Me, let him deny himself, and take up his cross, and follow Me."

In a kingdom, the king owns it all, thus in God's Kingdom, God owns it all.

Moses begins his instructions in Deuteronomy with God saying, "See, I have set the land before you; go in and possess the land which the Lord swore to your fathers – to Abraham, Isaac, and Jacob – to give to them and their descendants after them.'" Deuteronomy 1:8

The earth is the Lord's, and all its fullness, the world and those who dwell therein. – Psalm 24:1

- **GOD WANTS YOU TO BE RULER OVER MANY THINGS.**

"His lord said to him, 'Well done, good and faithful servant; you were faithful over a few things, I will make you ruler over many things. Enter the joy of your lord. – Matthew 25:21

- **NO AMOUNT IS TOO SMALL FOR GOD TO OWN.**

And He looked up and saw the rich putting their gifts into the treasury, and He saw also a certain poor widow putting in two mites. So He said, "Truly I say to you that this poor widow has put in more than all; for all these out of their abundance have put in offerings for God, but she out of her poverty put in all the livelihood that she had." – Luke 21:1-4

- **ACTION IS REQUIRED BY THE STEWARD.**

"Then he who had received the one talent came and said, 'Lord, I knew you to be a hard man, reaping where you have not sown, and gathering where you have not scatted seed. And I was afraid, and went and hid your talent in the ground. Look, there you have what is yours'. "But his lord answered and said to him, 'You wicked and lazy servant, you knew that I reap where I have not sown, and gather where I have not scattered seed. 'So you ought to have deposited my money with the bankers, and at my coming I would have received back my own with interest. Therefore take the talent from him, and give [it] to him who has ten talents. 'For to everyone who has, more will be given, and he will have abundance; but from him who does not have, even what he has will be taken away. 'And cast the unprofitable servant into the outer darkness. There will be weeping and gnashing of teeth.' – Matthew 25:24-30

Stewardship and Your Faithfulness – Since stewardship is a part of our servant/king relationship with God, faithfulness is required. We know that an unfaithful servant is not a servant at all; likewise, an unfaithful steward is not a steward.

- **BE FAITHFUL, IT IS REQUIRED.**

  Moreover it is required in stewards that one be found faithful. – 1 Corinthians 4:2

- **BE FAITHFUL WITH ALL OF YOUR RESOURCES.**

  Honor the Lord with your possessions, and the first fruits of your increase; so your barns will be filled with plenty, and your vats will overflow with new wine. – Proverbs 3:9-10

- **BE FAITHFUL IN LITTLE THINGS, REGARDLESS OF HOW MUCH YOU HAVE.**

  You must demonstrate productivity in the natural before you are given more spiritual territory. Before you walk in God's abundance, you must demonstrate faithfulness with little. Why should you ask God for more on your plate when you are demonstrating that you can't handle what you have? "

  He who is faithful in what is least is faithful also in much; and he who is unjust in what is least is unjust also in much. – Luke 16:10

- **BE FAITHFUL WITH ANOTHER'S POSSESSIONS.**

  Your vision will not come to pass until you make someone else's vision come to pass.

  And if you have not been faithful in what is another man's, who will give you what is your own." – Luke 16:12

Stewardship and Your Attitude – Your attitude determines your action. Therefore, in order to be a steward, you must never view money as an end in itself, but merely as a resource used to accomplish Kingdom goals and obligations as outlined by God. You must trust God here just as you trust Him with your eternity. The parable of the unjust steward (Luke 16:1-13) teaches us that we will be held accountable for what God puts into our lives to manage and that we cannot waste God's deposit into our lives.

God will recall the investment that He has put into you and take it back! Like the steward who tried to scheme and 'get over' on his master, we cannot deceive or defraud God. He will use life's circumstances and situations to expose what's in our hearts:

> *Now the Pharisees, who were lovers of money, also heard all these things, and they derided Him. And He said to them, "You are those who justify yourselves before men, but God knows your hearts. For what is highly esteemed among men is an abomination in the sight of God. – Luke 16:14-15*

Your Attitude About Money

1. You can't serve God and money! Love and loyalty go hand in hand!

> *No one can serve two masters; for either he will hate the one and love the other, or else he will be loyal to the one and despise the other. You cannot serve God and mammon." – Matthew 6:24*

2. Real life is not measured by how much you own.

> *And He said to them, "Take heed and beware of covetousness, for one's life does not consist in the abundance of the things he possesses." – Luke 12:15*

3. Be careful about your desire to be rich!

But those who desire to be rich fall into temptation and a snare, and into many foolish and harmful lusts which drown men in destruction and perdition. For the love of money is a root of all kinds of evil, for which some have strayed from the faith in their greediness, and pierced themselves through with many sorrows. – 1 Timothy 6:9-10

4. You can't take it with you when you die! Humans have tried to gain and keep dominion over God's resources since the beginning of time. The Egyptians tried to take it with them and were buried with all their worldly treasures. Don't let that which is accumulated have influence over you.

And he said: "Naked I came from my mother's womb, and naked shall I return there. The Lord gave, and the Lord has taken away; blessed be the name of the Lord." – Job 1:21

Your Attitude About Debt

1. Borrower is servant to the lender.

The rich rules over the poor, and the borrower is servant to the lender. – Proverbs 22:7

2. Owe no man anything except to love one another.

Owe no one anything except to love one another, for he who loves another has fulfilled the law. – Romans 13:8

3. It is considered part of the curse for disobedience.

"The alien who is among you shall rise higher and higher above you, and you shall come down lower and lower. He shall lend to you, but you shall not lend to him; he shall be the head, and you shall be the tail. – Deuteronomy 28:43-44

4. The wicked borrow and don't pay back.

The wicked borrows and does not repay, but the righteous shows mercy and gives. – Psalm 37:21

Different Attitudes About Money			
	Poverty	**Prosperity**	**Stewardship**
Possessions are:	Evil	A right	A responsibility
I work to:	Meet only basic needs	Become rich	Serve Christ
Godly people are:	Poor	Wealthy	Faithful
Ungodly people are:	Wealthy	Poor	Unfaithful
I give:	Because I must	To get	Because I love God
My spending is:	Without gratitude to God	Carefree and consumptive	Prayerful and responsible

Stewardship and Your Future – Have you maximized everything you have to perpetuate the Kingdom? As a steward, just like any other servant, you have to give an account of what you have been given charge over. You must give an account of everything God has given you.

*   Information – Teach your children about God's perspective about stewardship.

   "You shall teach them diligently to your children, and shall talk of them when you sit in your house, when you walk by the way, when you lie down, and when you rise up. – Deuteronomy 6:7

- Inheritance – Leave an inheritance for your children's children.

A good man leaves an inheritance to his children's children, but the wealth of the sinner is stored up for the righteous. – Proverbs 13:22

- Investing – Spend less than you earn. Save and invest the difference over a long period of time, because investing requires diligence, study and counsel. (Please inquiring about my online School of Financial Training and my GPS (Growing Prosperity Systematically) Handbooks of Financial Intelligence).

The plans of the diligent lead surely to plenty, but those of everyone who is hasty, surely to poverty. – Proverbs 21:5

Stewardship and Your Reward – Good stewardship has its rewards. God promises that if we are faithful stewards over what we have, God will reward us by making us stewards over more things (Matthew 25:23).

So be a good steward and receive:

- The increase!
  Gather little by little and your money will grow! In other words, spend less that you earn and do it for a long time, and you will be financially successful.

  ...but he who gathers by labor will increase. – Proverbs 13:11b

- The true riches!
  God wants to entrust to you, not just material possessions, but the truth of the gospel! Stewardship affects your relationship with God and your witness.

  "Therefore if you have not been faithful in the unrighteous mammon, who will commit to your trust the true riches?" – Luke 16:11

The Kingdom Tax

The tithe is the main tax of the Kingdom that influences the sustainability of the embassy the church and its staff. Now that you understand what stewardship is all about, it is important to understand the significance of tithing and giving offerings. As a Christian, you must give an account for how you conduct yourself in this life, especially as it relates to your finances. In the Old Testament, the tithe is defined as *ma`aser* (mah-as-ayr') or the tenth part – payment of a tenth part.

Tithing Before the Law
Before Moses and the Ten Commandments, Abraham tithed to Melchizedek out of respect.

> *Then Melchizedek king of Salem brought out bread and wine; he was the priest of God Most High. And he blessed him and said: "Blessed be Abram of God Most High, possessor of heaven and earth; and blessed be God Most High, who has delivered your enemies into your hand." And he gave him a tithe of all. – Genesis 14:18-20*

Tithing and the Law
In the Mosaic Law, the purpose of the tithe was to take care of the house of God. God's Kingdom has always existed on the tithe. The Bible declares that a tithe belongs to the Lord. The tithe was instituted on everything the Israelites had, and God gave instructions to add 20 percent when you did tithe, but were late. Similarly, just as the tax supports the natural government and taxes provide resources for the natural government to function and provide key services, so the tithe provides resources for the Kingdom to function.

> *"Speak thus to the Levites, and say to them: 'When you take from the children of Israel the tithes which I have given you from them as your inheritance, then you shall offer up a heave offering of it to the LORD, a tenth of the tithe'. – Numbers 18:26*

Bring all the tithes into the storehouse, that there may be food in My house. – Malachi 3:10a

'And all the tithe of the land, whether of the seed of the land or of the fruit of the tree, is the Lord's. It is holy to the Lord. If a man wants at all to redeem any of his tithes, he shall add one-fifth to it. And concerning the tithe of the herd or the flock, of whatever passes under the rod, the tenth one shall be holy to the Lord. – Leviticus 27:30-32

Tithing Today

Since tithing didn't start with the law, it doesn't end with the law either. Jesus paid the Pharisees very few compliments, but the one compliment he gave was about their tithing.

"Woe to you, scribes and Pharisees, hypocrites! For you pay tithe of mint and anise and cummin, and have neglected the weightier matters of the law: justice and mercy and faith. These you ought to have done, without leaving the others undone. – Matthew 23:23

If Christ disparaged the tithe, this would have been a wonderful time to do it but instead He encouraged it. The tithe is not attached to Judaism and the temple, but it is attached to the concept of a local representation (embassy) and mission center. It is interesting that there is no other relationship that exists where people do not have financial accountability, including a marriage. God calls people that violate the Kingdom principles of accountability – robbers (Malachi 3:10). The Kingdom citizen cannot engage in illegal activities that violate the principles of the Kingdom.

Chapter Seven:
The Kingdom Drivers – The Building Blocks of Citizenry

Now that we have been introduced to the basic tenets and features of the Kingdom, we want to explore now how each Kingdom citizen is to function within the parameters and principles of the Kingdom. I call them the Kingdom drivers. Why? Because I believe these are the features and basic tenets that drive the operations of the Kingdom through the embassy or church. By now, you should be well convinced and familiar with the basic concept of the Kingdom and the message of the Kingdom. You should understand how to see the Kingdom, how to enter the Kingdom, and how to seek the Kingdom. But the question is now mentality. The Kingdom drivers are designed to assist you in developing a Kingdom mentality. We are called to think Kingdom! Christ was totally inundated with the Kingdom, and the Bible instructs us to let that mind that was in Christ Jesus also be in us. The mind of Christ was a Kingdom mentality, so if you are going to function as a full-fledged Kingdom citizen and minister, you must understand the basic drivers of the Kingdom.

What is My Prerequisite Knowledge?

Before you learn how the Kingdom operates, you have to understand what you're dealing with. If you bought a new car and wanted to know how to drive it, you'd have to become familiar with the rules of the road; the features of the car; and the operator components like the steering wheel, pedals, gear shifter, side and rear view mirrors and seat controls. Basically, before you even get to the operational stage, you have to have some prerequisite knowledge.

There are seven characteristics that drive Kingdom functionality and its operation. Each and every element is essential and must be recognized, fully understood, and mentally and spiritually embraced if you are going to be a Kingdom citizen. Each element is predicated on the preceding element; they are the building blocks for the citizenry.

The Kingdom drivers and building blocks are:

- Sovereignty – The understanding that God is supreme and answers to no one.
- Stewardship – The understanding that everything belongs to God and ultimately returns to Him and we are simply managers of His resources.
- Structure – The understanding that the Kingdom operates from a governmental structure and is not random.
- Servanthood – The understanding that our lives belong to God and it is a privilege to have Him as King.
- Sacrifice – The understanding that we are called to become living sacrifices that deny ourselves and choices for the expansion of the Kingdom of God and this is simply our reasonable service.
- Submission – This is the understanding that we are called to obey God with a cheerful spirit rather we agree or not.
- Sonship – This is the understanding that we are sons of God which means we have a deep covenant relationship with God that makes Him responsible for us as His children. This also carries the fact that only sons can inherit from the King of Kings.

Let's explore the seven drivers and building blocks to your Kingdom citizenry.

1. Sovereignty

During the life of Christ and in the centuries following, kingdoms were much more prevalent and powerful than we can imagine. In current times, there are only seven absolute monarchies – Bhutan, Brunei, Oman, Qatar, Saudi Arabia, Swaziland, and Vatican City, which is also a theocracy. In our western culture, we give absolutely no credence to these geographies and rarely are exposed to this form of government. We all know that England has a queen, but we also understand that the prime minister is elected and that person interacts with the people as a governmental leader. Monarchies mean nothing.

134

This is the democratized concept of sovereignty, referred to as "popular sovereignty", where the populace possesses some level of sovereignty, and the government is a representative democracy administered by elected officials. This is a paradigm that is ingrained in our unsaved nature, because it is all we have known for our entire lives. We vote for everything, starting at very young ages when we vote on what movie to see with our families or who wins the teacher of the year award. Then, as we approach high school, we begin to participate in school government. In college, we may join the young Democrats or young Republicans. Ultimately, we take pride in participating in the electoral process, because our earthly heritage proclaims the fact that people died to establish the right to vote. However, we need to examine the issue of sovereignty, which differs from what we know. Sovereignty is the exclusive right to exercise supreme authority over a geographic region, group of people, or oneself. A sovereign is the supreme lawmaking authority, subject to no other. This is chief unquestionable rule; not a democracy, no church vote. The Bible does not ask for your opinion.

Throughout our Christian walk, or even for those who are simply exposed to church services, Christ is preached as King with a secondary subtlety to His role as savior. If you can be frank, rarely do we focus on what it means to be subject to the King. Even in our salvific experience, we accept Christ as our Savior (verb) who paid a ransom for our lives with His blood. We also accept Him as Lord (noun) or one who governs. Most of us, by default, think of Him as a savior who saves, not actually our Lord who rules and reigns over us. But in reality, Christ IS first the Lord who saves. We cannot dichotomize this relationship and still expect to go to heaven; when we can't recognize His sovereignty in our earthly lives. It's a prerequisite to accepting the offer of salvation. It is not possible to live in a Kingdom where the King does not govern. Kings do not ask subjects for their opinions.

The democratization of Christianity began to occur in 394 AD, and the church underwent a governmental change mirroring the republic and democratic rule (of the people, for the people, by the people). But the Kingdom of heaven should be mirroring a monarchy with theocratic rule. Offices in the church became determined by popular vote vs. royal appointments, which God had preordained. These are diametrically opposite ends of the spectrum for governance. In one instance, everyone has a voice, but in the Kingdom, only God has the voice.

The integration of the church with civil government led to the establishment of a further confusion that has ingrained itself in our society, that of the apostolic, which will be examined in the next section.

Isaiah 9:7 states:

> *Of the increase of His government and peace there will be no end, Upon the throne of David and over His kingdom, To order it and establish it with judgment and justice From that time forward, even forever. The zeal of the Lord of hosts will perform this.*

God Himself is bringing to pass His sovereign rule through Christ. God's rule is a certainty; He is going to manifest His will and purpose as He sees fit.

Paul states this in Romans 8:14-17:

> *For as many as are led by the Spirit of God, these are sons of God. For you did not receive the spirit of bondage again to fear, but you received the Spirit of adoption by whom we cry out, "Abba, Father." The Spirit Himself bears witness with our spirit that we are children of God, and if children, then heirs--heirs of God and joint heirs with Christ, if indeed we suffer with [Him], that we may also be glorified together.*

God is just…not fair. The question for us, therefore, is simple. Will we enter the Kingdom of God? Will we come UNDER God's rule? The question is whether we will turn to Christ and be governed by Him according to the principles required for Kingdom operation. These principles operate with parameters, purposes, and periods.

2. Stewardship

The Kingdom driver of stewardship was discussed in detail under the chapter – Kingdom Economy. However, in this section, I want to emphasize not the rule of stewardship, but the intrinsic value of stewardship.

We are stewards of God's resources, but we forget what a privilege it is to be given God's resources to take care and use for our sustenance and pleasure. Out of sheer gratitude, we should feel the overwhelming unction to give back to God whatever He asks in light of what He has entrusted to us. And then as we reflect on the magnitude of what God has given (even His only Son), reciprocation should automatically be accompanied with willingness and cheerfulness.

David's prayer of praise is one Kingdom citizens should reflect on daily:

> *Therefore David blessed the LORD before all the assembly; and David said: "Blessed are You, LORD God of Israel, our Father, forever and ever. Yours, O LORD, is the greatness, the power and the glory, the victory and the majesty; For all that is in heaven and in earth is Yours; Yours is the kingdom, O LORD, and You are exalted as head over all. Both riches and honor come from You, and You reign over all. In Your hand is power and might; In Your hand it is to make great and to give strength to all. "Now therefore, our God, we thank You and praise Your glorious name. But who am I, and who are my people, that we should be able to offer so willingly as this? For all things come from You, and of Your own we have given You. For we are aliens and pilgrims before You, as were all our fathers; Our days on earth are as a shadow, and without hope. – 1 Chronicles 29:10-15*

Yet, God is just. We must be mindful of God's expectations of man to be a faithful and productive steward who carefully watches over and increases that which He has placed in our lives. These expectations are hidden in the Kingdom parables on stewardship:

Stewardship Parables		
Parable of...	Scripture Reference	Stewardship Focus
The Wise and Foolish Virgins	Matthew 25:1-13	We should be wise and careful stewards of our covenant relationship with God.
The Lost Coin	Luke 15:8-10	We should be wise and careful stewards of our covenant relationship with God.
The Talents	Matthew 25:14-30	Regardless of the size, God expects us to be productive stewards over the things of value He places in our possession.
The Minas	Luke 19:11-27	Those who are faithful stewards will be rewarded. Those who are unfaithful will be punished.

Each of these parables is given as a lesson and is meant to forewarn believers of the coming evaluation of our stewardship. The Bible tells us that all believers must appear at the Judgment Seat of Christ (2 Corinthians 5:10-11; 1 Corinthians 3:11-15). This is not a judgment regarding our salvation. Rather, this judgment will be God's audit of how we managed all that He placed in our lives.

3. Structure

When God establishes an entity, organization, or institution in the scripture, He did so by establishing order. The number 12 is the number of government, establishment, and order. The number 12 is very significant in biblical numerology. The number 12 is frequently the divisor for astronomical and astrological principles. The moon undergoes 12 full cycles in the course of approximately one solar year; 12 months establish and govern the whole year. The day is also divided into two 12-hour periods. In the Anglo-Saxon system of measurement, there are 12 inches in a foot, and 12 units in a dozen. Ten fingers plus two hands equals 12. In some Jewish or Hebraic thought, they also consider the fact that the multiplication of the very special numbers three, which is:

- Symbol of balance
- The reconciliation of opposites
- Completeness
- The three ancestral patriarchs: Abraham, Isaac, and Jacob;
- Three major pilgrimages: Passover, Shavuot, and Sukkot;
- Three major divisions of Bible: Torah, Prophets, and Writings, etc.

and four, associated with:

- The earth and its rhythms
- Four corners
- Four seasons
- Four directions
- Four winds
- Four elements
- Four rivers in that flowed through the garden
- The Tetragrammaton

equals 12!

In addition, the sum of the two equals seven, which also seems to be a significant number in biblical numerology. Adding the number five (5, which is the number of grace, fingers, toes, extremities, Torah, protection) plus seven (7, the number of completion) also equals 12. The male descendants of Adam listed in Genesis 4:1-26 numbered 12. When God established the Old Testament covenant with Israel, He established her based upon the principle of the 12 with the 12 tribes of Israel. Ancient Israel was divided into 12 tribes under which they were established and governed. Twelve is the number of government and order, such that there were 12 jewels in breastplate of the priests, 12 rods were used to establish the priesthood under Aaron (tribe of Levi).

Jesus began teaching at the age of 12. When He established the church or the New Testament covenant community, He did so based upon the 12 disciples; these 12 disciples established and governed the Kingdom movement of Christ. Twelve was such an important number that He personally replaced Judas with the Apostle Paul (He did not chose Matthias). Thus, in eschatology, there will be 12 apostles in the New Jerusalem, and there will be 12 gates to the city. Coincidence? Absolutely not.

The Kingdom of God is structured by relationships, and God has an order for the relationships in His Kingdom. The Kingdom is a theocracy; thus, God sends delegated officials to represent His interests as His official messengers (*shuluach* in Hebrew). This is why Isaiah was as a messenger of God. He had the power of attorney in order to execute in the stead of Him who sent him. The Talmud states that a man's *shuluach* is as the man himself. His authority can extend to standing proxy in marriage. Though the marriage was official, the limitation was that he could not consummate or have sex with the bride. God governs His Kingdom through delegated leadership who represent Him and lead the people. We refer to this concept as the apostolic. The head of Christ is God the Father, the head of man is Christ, and the head of woman is man.

This is an example of apostolic order listed in 1 Corinthians 11:3. Christ is the head of the church (Ephesians 1:22); and He has appointed these in the church, first apostles, secondly prophets, and thirdly teachers, etc. The King established order based upon reflection; thus, apostolic order entails reflecting the image of God, not the personal or individual wishes of a person.

The commonly accepted use of the term "apostolic" often refers to the patristic writings of the early church fathers as apostolic writings. The term is designed to connote (1) authority and (2) connection to the early church. What was the mission of the early church? Their mission was to preach the Kingdom of God and God's perfect will; we are in the dispensation of theological renewal that demands the gospel of the Kingdom be preached – so we must live in that which we obediently evangelize to others about.

God does everything with order; He is a God of order and quality, not chaos, the author of peace not confusion, as stated in 1 Corinthians 14:33a. As the God of structure, He establishes order through appropriate placement; everything and everyone in its place. The first principle established in creation was order. In Genesis chapter one, God brought order out of chaos. He ordered light from darkness; separated water, sky, and land (v. 1-9). God then set parameters based on purpose – aside from the creation of vegetation and inhabitation which were purposefully made to reproduce after their kind; He created the sun and the moon to mark the distinctions of time.

This requirement for order extends to the secular world. In academia, you are given your syllabus, class expectations, and requirements for materials that ultimately determine your outcome. At work, if the requirements for corporate order that exist are ignored, you will not work there for long. If the governmental rules that have been established for you to occupy your place in society are ignored, they have a special cell with your name on it.

Similarly, in God's Kingdom, there are consequences for being out of order. Since He established order and structure, there are lines of accountability and authority. Therefore, whatever the task may be in the Kingdom, there must be clear lines of authority and consistent accountability to ensure that expectations and responsibilities are executed in a timely manner with precision. Matthew 6:10 states:

Your kingdom come, Your will be done on earth as it is in heaven.

In teaching us how to pray with the model prayer, Jesus makes it clear that God's will is already being done in heaven, so it's a must that His will be sought in earnest in order for His Kingdom to manifest on earth.

God's structure, as befitting His sovereignty, does not give any weight to how you feel about any other person or the task at hand. Positional authority demands appropriate responses, regardless of your feelings. Kingdom order is modeled in the natural as a mirror of Christ's monarchy. For instance, if you have ever been to court, you know that it does not matter that the judge is a person just like you are. The judge sets the standard of behavior in his court; you refer to him as 'your honor' and you speak when you're spoken to or you're out of order and might go directly to jail!

We know from our discussion of sovereignty that God reigns supreme, through His Son, Jesus Christ. His reign is designed to be the rule over the hearts and lives of people, and you cannot honor the King if you do not honor His structure. How do we translate this spiritual Kingdom in our hearts into tangible citizenship? The Kingdom of God is structured by relationships – at every level. Let's take a look at the rule of the Kingdom structure.

The Church as the Embassy

The Kingdom of God is administrated through embassies. An embassy is a better model of what Christ and the 1st century church evangelized and discipled through than what the "church" has evolved into, as we learned in our lesson about the Kingdom and the church. The embassy represents the kingdom in another land and establishes the king's territory on foreign soil with a diplomatic mission. Embassies are envoys to these foreign regions offering peace and hope for a mutually beneficial relationship with the government they represent. The Kingdom of heaven is manifested in this world, but Satan is the king of this cosmos or earthly inhabitation; thus, our embassies are beacons and havens from the one who comes to steal, kill, and destroy.

There is only one embassy in any foreign nation that governs the implementation of the king's policies and establishes the satellite consulates that will serve the outer areas of that foreign nation. In the outlying areas, consulates perform a highly critical, yet basic function for the kingdom. They issue visas and passports for those sojourning in their region of the world, help foreigners with the process of changing their citizenship, and represent their leadership as shiningly proud examples of patriotic pride. These subordinate offices see to the needs of the travelers in a foreign land and, in the instances where citizens of the host country want what you have, they will come to the embassy or consulate seeking a life change.

Kingdom citizens are in this world, but not of it, as Jesus defined for us in His prayer for the disciples in John 17:14-16. However, while under the authority of the embassy, Kingdom citizens enjoy the same privileges and rights as if they were in heaven. We are protected only when we are part of the covering of an embassy, either directly or through a consulate office whose duly appointed emissaries are our direct intermediaries with the King.

These emissaries have a direct authority line to the King through the ambassador and his consulates (local churches or ministries). Within each consulate's span of responsibility are travelers who are permanently assigned to that region of the world. In our paradigm, the individual households are 'travelers' assigned to the consulates that are living a Kingdom life as Kingdom citizens under the rule and authority of their consulates and embassies. The consulate makes sure that people in that area can access the King.

Further delegation of structure in individual households must also exist. Thus the head of man is woman, and the children are subject to them. Kingdom homes must reflect spiritual structure within their homes and comply with the spiritual structure in God's house. For the masses of Kingdom citizens, a Holy Spirit-filled, biblically-run household is the first-order group under leadership that is accountable to obedience to God's sovereign structure. The internal hierarchy in the home is God, Christ, strong man, and submissive woman who can then bear and raise Kingdom citizens.

Embassy Structure

In order to execute His reign on earth, within the established embassies, God has set up a hierarchy of spiritual management. In fact, God demands order. This is accomplished through spiritual governance by the person God has placed in authority. The offices of the church are explicitly defined in 1 Corinthians 12:28,

> *And God has appointed these in the church: first apostles, second prophets, third teachers, after that miracles, then gifts of healings, helps, administrations, varieties of tongues.*

The most misunderstood office, and least discussed in the 21st century, is the apostle.

The relationship of everyone in the Kingdom to the apostles is key to the Kingdom structure actually working and the orders of the King's mandate, evangelism and discipleship, to be effectively implemented with the vision that God is casting, through these ambassadors, for His people.

Apostles are spiritually gifted in all of the areas common to the prophet, pastor, teacher, and evangelist but evangelists, teachers, pastors, and prophets are NOT apostles. While others may also have the spiritual impartation of healing, tongues and prophesy, those gifted to heal, speak in tongues, or prophesy are NOT apostles. In the same way that apostles are gifted with the gifts of people who hold other subordinate church offices, the apostle will have established spiritual authority in his household and also will have walked efficiently in the role of shepherd or consulate head. See the relative order of these gifts and callings in the Kingdom structure diagram below. Structure is recognizable because it is visible and tangible. The authority flows within the structure, and the purposes of the individual components are depicted below.

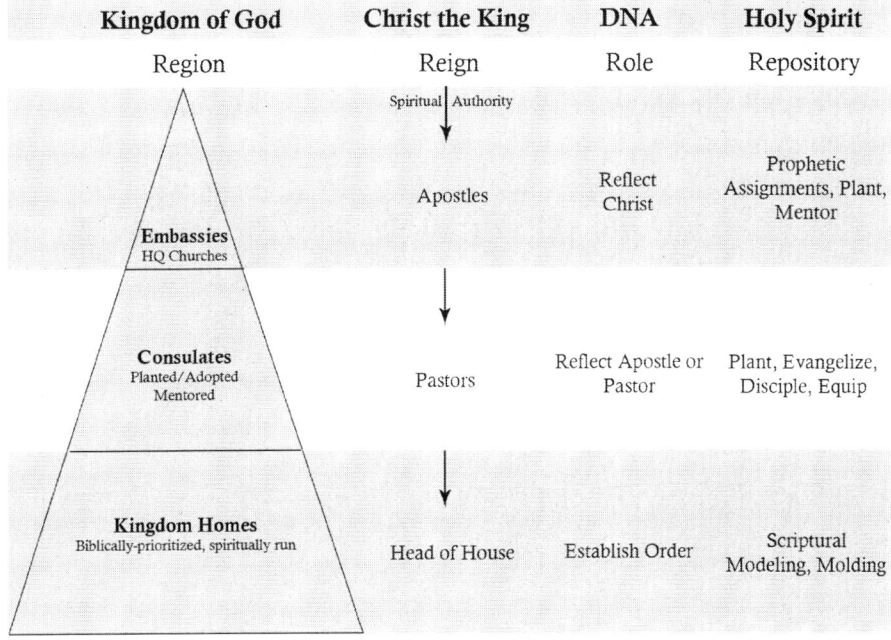

Kingdom of God	Christ the King	DNA	Holy Spirit
Region	Reign	Role	Repository
	Spiritual Authority		
Embassies HQ Churches	Apostles	Reflect Christ	Prophetic Assignments, Plant, Mentor
Consulates Planted/Adopted Mentored	Pastors	Reflect Apostle or Pastor	Plant, Evangelize, Disciple, Equip
Kingdom Homes Biblically-prioritized, spiritually run	Head of House	Establish Order	Scriptural Modeling, Molding

"Church order", with trustees and deacon boards governing the body, is unscriptural; deacons are not called to authority, they're called to serve! There are people walking in spiritual influence over others with no anointing or biblical precedent. Democracy in the church leaves feelings of disgruntlement, based on accusations of manipulation of power through lobbying, cronyism, and division. Our current government is proof of the effects of democratic problems in governance.

In terms of recognizing the role of apostle/ambassador in the historical church, there is no controversy. Traditional dispensationalists, theologians who have a very specific perception of the successive epochs of theology, teach that the era of the apostle ended with the 12 apostles. Nowhere in the Bible does it state or infer that the role of the apostle was eliminated or would cease to be needed. While no one will have the unction (specific anointing) of the original apostles who walked with Jesus, or of the biblical writer Paul, whose Damascus road experience provided him with his divine calling, history is filled with "apostles". We need to examine this in order to understand our own role in the Kingdom.

Apostle means "one who is sent to establish". As Christ's church spread throughout the world, there have been people of note that did not refer to themselves as apostles during their own lifetimes, but that's exactly what they were. Consider Martin Luther, whose 95 Theses spoke out against indulgences or repentance through works, which were being granted wholesale by the Roman Catholic Church. He was sent. The historical record now reflects the impact Luther had on ushering in the Dispensation of Salvation. In the same way, John Calvin, John Wesley, as well as, William J. Seymour established great things for God and were sent. Each and every denomination was established by someone God spoke to and gave a vision. These men were usually operating completely outside the scope of traditional religious thought and the current application of theology.

Apostles are anointed and ordained by the Holy Spirit and their purpose and office is divinely imparted and supported. God sends apostles to manifest His preordained will in the time and season that He sees fit. In fact, God has always raised up a leader for every significant move or transition with His people. God's consistency in raising up leaders for a move by imparting them with vision from the Holy Spirit based on biblical examples, for example: Moses – move the people out of Egypt, Joshua – move Israel into the Promised Land, David – move the people under a king after God's own heart. Being "sent" is not synonymous with being perfect. God uses flawed men. Moses listened to the people and stopped executing the vision; David was covetous and adulterous, yet they were all sent.

This brings us to the 21st century and the Kingdom of God. The theology is not new, Jesus preached this. God is not opening the canon or scripture; He is imparting the power of the Holy Spirit to usher in a significant move in the express fulfillment of His word – and God is using His ambassadors to affect His policy implementation. But the timing with which God has chosen to move, or usher in theological renewal, means that right now historically significant apostles have been and are being sent. Apostles are commanded to establish apostolic order under the covering of their authority, which is imparted directly from the Holy Spirit. His mission is to strategically move the people of God forward towards the renewing of God's ordained theology by recognizing and fulfilling their individual purposes.

The confluence of gifts in the apostle begins with his vision for ministry. God then calls people to him and as Kingdom citizens, or as consulate heads, each with a divine purpose that falls into alignment with the fulfillment of the apostle's God-ordained mission. All things will be working together for good (Romans 8:28) to realize the vision all over the world under apostles which we have yet to know.

1. **The apostolic creates order in the embassy or church, and order creates peace with God to give others hope.**

Romans 14:17 says:

... for the kingdom of God is not eating and drinking, but righteousness, peace, and joy in the Holy Spirit.

This translates to the apostolic order being essential for the Kingdom of God on earth. The apostolic is the governmental authority in the embassy, or church, just as it was when Christ had 12 disciples, or learners, who He sent forth to establish His church in accordance with Kingdom principles.

2. **The role of the apostolic is to be the authority that aligns you to your purpose in the Kingdom.**

If you are going to be a Kingdom citizen operating in obedience, and not a church member, then you must understand that God has a time and space for everyone and everything. Prophetic alignment is more than just assisting people with the selfish goal of being ministered to; it is ensuring that you are aligned with God's times and seasons in your life. If you try and force issues, you will mess up your life, because your purpose is time sensitive. Many people join church, and no one is asking, "God, where do You want me? Is this church under apostolic covering? What does this church teach and preach? What is the vision and mission of this church? What is the quality of its training ministry?" These are questions that Kingdom-minded ministries can answer and respond to in a very sound manner.

God sends the apostle with your prophetic assignment! Many people claim to have known their call all of their lives, even before salvation. Those desires are based on fleshly talents; you must be careful of mistaking talents for gifts and careers for callings. You also must take care of the ungoverned spiritual "giftings"; they can mislead and send you right to hell!

God is not looking for gifted people; He is looking for called people. You can not live in the Kingdom without purpose, and God will define your purpose by where you fit in His overall plan. Your apostle, or ministry gift, will help you find your fit in the body that is connected to your purpose. Remember that Kingdom citizens are conceived with purpose. Ephesians 1:4 confirms:

> *...just as He chose us in Him before the foundation of the world, that we should be holy and without blame before Him in love...*

3. The apostle establishes doctrine, plants churches, and trains leaders.

Anyone, who God sends to operate in the apostolic as an ambassador, will be highly skilled in the three areas of doctrine, church planting, and leadership training and development. Why? To answer four pertinent questions in Romans 10:14 -15a:

> *How then shall they call on Him in whom they have not believed? And how shall they believe in Him of whom they have not heard? And how shall they hear without a preacher? And how shall they preach unless they are sent?*

Apostles are shepherds, but shepherds are not necessarily apostles. Every Kingdom Christian should be under a covering; there should be a shepherd over each and every spiritual life. The apostle is God's chosen person of governmental Kingdom authority and is designed to watch for your spiritual life. If you do not know who you're called to, you're out of order; if you do know and don't obey, you're out of order.

Apostles will speak into the lives and ministries of the pastors of the embassy's consulates with their purpose! In 2 Timothy 2:2, it says:

> *And the things that you have heard from me among many witnesses, commit these to faithful men who will be able to teach others also.*

The Bible speaks to the entire fellowship of believers, when encountering those who had been sent, in Acts 2:42:

And they continued steadfastly in the apostles' doctrine and fellowship, in the breaking of bread, and in prayers.

Finally, apostles bring order and establish a "work" of ministry, as a result of their vision.

And we know that all things work together for good to those who love God, to those who are the called according to His purpose.

In Romans 8:28, it uses the Greek word *sunergeo*. The *erg-* root is also in the word "ergonomics" today. The apostle will ensure that God's vision is brought about in a manner that ensures efficient use of resources.

4. **As shepherds, along with teaching these skills to the consular heads, their charge is to:**

   - Lay the foundation (Hebrews 6:1-2) and
   - Equip you for faithful service (Ephesians 4:12) – opportunity to serve in ministry

Ministry is about serving other people, not doing what you like to do with people you like to do it with. If it is not serving someone who does not know Christ, through evangelism or discipleship, it is not Kingdom service as defined by the apostle's teaching of the Word. The structure of the relationships, beginning with Christ's special anointing of the apostle, to the apostle's relationship with the spiritual leaders under him, as well as the direct citizens in the embassy, the relationships of the citizens with one another, relationships with those in the same household, and finally each individual's relationship with Christ must be defined by the Word of God from beginning to end!

4. Servanthood

Structure does not work without a servant's mentality. Christ is a King, but in His earthly walk, He modeled servanthood and the mentality that accompanies it. Christ was consumed with His "Father's business", and so we must be. Often times, church people confuse "good works" with service to the King. You cannot serve on your terms; you must serve in the capacity that you're called to, or you are out of order.

In John 13:1-17, we see Jesus' model of servanthood in the example of washing the disciples' feet. At this point, His followers were learners, so in everything Christ did, He was teaching. Peter reacted with shock, because this was a lowly task – washing the day's grime from a person's feet. Jesus tells him (and us) in verse 7:

> *"What I am doing you do not understand now, but you will know after this."*

This is our lesson as well, for Christ goes on to say in vv. 13-15, in response to Peter's shock and reluctance that Christ wash his hands and head:

> *"You call Me Teacher and Lord, and you say well, for so I am. If I then, your Lord and Teacher, have washed your feet, you also ought to wash one another's feet. For I have given you an example, that you should do as I have done to you. Most assuredly, I say to you, a servant is not greater than his master; nor is he who is sent greater than he who sent him.*

As is in keeping with Kingdom order, Christ noted that the offices of servant, master, Lord, and teacher are not dismissed because of the fact that Kingdom citizens are called to servanthood and a servant's attitude. Referring to the diagram of structure, you are called to your service in all of the areas under which you fall in your life. Within your home, if you are the head of the house, you are called to your purpose there.

You have to be taught, willingly and with fervor, and then you have to apply what you have been taught in your home. In your consulate, you also have a purpose, and you must seek, serve, and sow into that ministry. You must maintain your alignment as governed by your apostle within. All of these structures set the parameters of your service.

The way in which you view Christ as Lord vs. Savior will affect your view of yourself as either a servant or one who is to be served. "Reflected" characteristics of Christ in leadership magnify how this is clearly the "inside out, upside down" difference between the Kingdom of God and the secular world. Kingdom of God leaders are truly servants of those in their charge.

We not only serve the King, we serve His court, others in the Kingdom, and more importantly, those for whom we offer entry into the Kingdom. In the Kingdom, the focus is not church attendance, but service. Scripture speaks of "serving," not services – as in church service. You are not performing a service by attending church or participating in any of the activities therein, unless it leads to evangelism and discipleship.

Models of Servanthood

In the Kingdom, we are to be models of servanthood, as Christ demonstrated. The citizens of the Kingdom are the custodians of the keys to the Kingdom. Christ is specific when He states that we should serve all those with whom we have relationships. If we are not modeling the appropriate action and attitude of servanthood, who is going to want the key to anything we have? Our interactions with another, as we live in two worlds, should be based on humility and grace and not on the secular relationship platform of external control.

As an example, in Matthew, Christ speaks to His own intrinsic nature of service when addressing a mother who wished her sons to be with Him in His Kingdom. Christ explained that lording authority over one another, even if that is your right, is not as it should be amongst those in the Kingdom. In Matthew 20:28, He concludes:

> *"...just as the Son of Man did not come to be served, but to serve, and give His life as a ransom for many."*

Christ performed the ultimate service and modeled rendering the most basic services to those around Him; this is one of the most easily seen differences in the Kingdom. Since it is not structured on the model of the secular world, there is no merit system. We are all saved by grace, so there is no "entitlement" that precludes service in any area whatsoever.

Paul opened his letter to the church at Rome, in 1:1 with:

> *Paul, a bondservant to Jesus Christ, called to be an apostle, separated to the gospel of God.*

The word used for "bondservant" is the Greek word *doulos*. A bondservant is one who is a slave by choice. He serves, because he chooses to be a slave. In ancient culture, this person could have worked and earned his freedom, but since his master had been so good to him, he realized that it was better to remain a slave. They would usually pierce his ear, and the earring was a visible sign that he was a bondservant. As a bondservant of Christ, we choose to be slaves.

What we have to realize is that the motivation for service is love – we love Him, because He first loved us, and that is enough for us to become willing bondservants. Service is not a requirement that can be 'met', therefore earning something or meeting a standard.

This is the legalism that Christ came to challenge in the Pharisees and what Martin Luther brought revival to during the Dispensation of Salvation. Service is a matter of grace, not legalism.

Jesus' primary commandment is that we love one another. That means that our service to our Kingdom purpose is coupled with our mandate to serve one another. God is not a respecter of persons. In the natural, people have ways in which they separate themselves, so that they are not one. In the Kingdom, there is no racism, sexism, classism, or any of the other "isms"; we are all saved by grace, so we are all spiritual equals and owe each other service (love). We should serve one another to further God's vision.

Usually we serve ourselves and our own purposes before we serve the purpose that God has established in our lives. We will prioritize everything in our lives, then come to 'church' and 'serve' in the choir. Our jobs, families, hobbies, social life, secular fulfillment will all come before the things of God. Working overtime to pay a car note and not being available to the service of the Lord, as is required to effectively fulfill your purpose in God's vision for your apostle's ministry, means you are subverting your service to the King. You are 'serving' treasure and trying to store up the world's, not God's, storehouse. And we know who the king of this world is!

One of the tricky areas for many Kingdom citizens, when it comes to service in the Kingdom, is your estimation of where your skills and talents should be used vs. where your spiritual authority has determined they should be directed. Giftings can take you out as a servant, because your will is to exercise your gift, but your call is to render your service. In the Kingdom, your service is to be rendered willingly and unrestrictedly to seeing, hearing, and manifesting your purpose. You must be willing to serve, or be as a slave, to your designated role in whatever brings the vision of God to pass.

The same humility it would take for you to wrap a towel around your midsection and literally wash the feet of your fellow (barefoot) sojourners, who have been traveling all day, is a willful action. Service is not attitude; it always requires action.

The critical element of service that takes you wanting to be served to being a bondservant is attitude. In Paul's case, he was not going about his service to the Lord unwillingly or begrudgingly. A slave does what he or she is told because of fear. Christians operating out of misplaced fear are not Kingdom citizens. Fear of hell, fear of death, fear of not being in the "church crowd", fear of how people will view you, fear of anything outside of God immediately turns your service into slavery.

Service is sometimes translated as "worship", as it is in the passage in Romans 12:1:

> "...present your bodies as a living sacrifice, holy and acceptable unto god, which is your reasonable service."

This text has applications throughout the nature of your service, as well as the next sections we will examine, sacrifice and submission; they are fused. But for our purposes, it is clear that the "reasonable service" here is to present yourself totally and completely to the will of God in your lives, after Kingdom structure puts you in the will of God and prophetically aligns you.

5. Sacrifice

For us, the question becomes "How?" How do we render service to the King? In order to serve, or render your actions in a manner that categorizes them under the heading of Kingdom service, you must sacrifice.

When Romans 12:1 speaks of a living sacrifice, which means we died to ourselves when we repented, our entire life is one lived on earth fulfilling our purpose in exchange for the sacrifice Christ made for us. Scripture says in Mark 8:34:

> *When He had called the people to Himself, with His disciples also, He said to them, "Whoever desires to come after Me, let him deny himself, and take up his cross, and follow Me.*

Those who serve must understand sacrifice. Denying yourself is hard, indeed. To live in the Kingdom, suddenly your priorities have taken a 180° turn. We have lived our entire lives, for the most part, prioritizing the things of this world. We strive for a secular education, and rightfully so, to fulfill a career based on our temperaments, talents, and training. But in the Kingdom, the priority is stated clearly in Matthew 6:33, when Jesus said:

> *But seek first the kingdom of God and His righteousness, and all these things shall be added to you.*

Seeking the Kingdom first means that your purpose in the Kingdom supersedes all of the things that you have been considering accomplishments based on what the secular world prioritizes. Your house, education, promotion potential, extra-curricular activities, and long-term financial freedom will not add to God's Kingdom. Basing your responses, desires, and tolerances on your Exacting Ezra, Pioneering Paul, Loving Leah, or People's Peter temperaments are not acceptable! You're finding yourself sacrificing just to walk in the Kingdom and you haven't started to help build the Kingdom!

A sacrifice is never something that is easily given; it does not come out of your excess, but in the Kingdom, neither does it cause poverty. If your priorities are still in the world, then yes, everything you give as your "reasonable service" to the King will be centered on fleshly priorities: "Where does this fit in my budget?"

"How can I do this and go to the fraternity/sorority meeting?" "How can I witness to someone I don't know?" "How can I labor alongside so-and-so to build the Kingdom – they irritate me?" "Well, I have to consider this promotion, even if that means I'll have to move to Indiana. My salary increase will be 50%!"

The Kingdom mentality dictates, not requests, your sacrifice. To be in order in the Kingdom, you must be willing to give up something unquestioningly and willingly, even if it does not fit your alignment, because it is in God's alignment and purposed to manifest His will. Sacrificing your life means surrendering or killing the things you hold dear: your agendas for your time, your talents, and your treasure. When you give your time, talents, and treasure, it should be over, above and outside that which you can rationalize. That's a sacrifice. But of course, you have died to yourself and your selfish desires, so you no longer feel pain based on expectations of the world. Remember, Romans 12:1 says that you, as a living sacrifice, are holy. You are set aside for your prophetically aligned purpose in the Kingdom. The key is that when you seek the Kingdom of God first, your priorities are in order. There is no question about what you must do and when – the vision to manifest the Kingdom will dictate it and you must give.

Not only must Kingdom citizens sacrifice, as directed, to fulfill the vision that encompasses their purpose in the Kingdom mission of evangelism and discipleship, it must be done cheerfully. In his second letter to the church at Corinth, Paul emphasizes this in chapter 9, verse 7. Here, we have verses 6-8 for context:

> *But this I say: He who sows sparingly will also reap sparingly, and he who sows bountifully will also reap bountifully. So let each one give as he purposes in his heart, not grudgingly or of necessity; for God loves a cheerful giver. And God is able to make all grace abound toward you, that you, always having all sufficiency in all [things], may have an abundance for every good work.*

You just have to love the consistency of the Kingdom's operational principles! We know from our discussion of servanthood that we are willing and freely giving ourselves in exchange for the sacrifice Jesus made when we made Him Lord. Paul addresses this by admonishing us that our service and sacrifice must not be reluctant. As Patti LaBelle says, "Don't block your blessings!"

6. Submission

Submission is not simply "obedience", it is obedience with the right attitude. In this obedience is your accountability to your covering. All operating structures have a system of accountability. Wherever there is structure and work to be done, you better believe the order is established to create accountability. On your jobs, obedience is enough. Just do what you're told, you can fake a good attitude – just get the work done and then you go home. But in the Kingdom, your ability to properly submit to the Lord Jesus Christ, and those who are in the position to watch over your soul, will determine whether or not you fulfill your purpose. The Kingdom is your spiritual home.

In the Kingdom, submission is not "works", which some confuse with service, because the ability to submit is completely against our independent fleshly nature. Jesus says in Mark 10:14b:

> "...Let the little children come to Me, and do not forbid them; for of such is the kingdom of God."

Children are submissive; even as they display rebellion and self-will in their growth. Parents must teach them to respect and honor authority as they mature or else their lack of order will have consequences. Deeply, children trust; it's easier for children to trust than adults who have suffered the disappointments and failed expectations of a life of the flesh. So, when we come to Christ with the submissive attitude of little children, we can perform with the trust in God that is manifest in our faith.

In the Kingdom, you fully rely on the King and, understanding God's sovereignty, you should have no expectation for your life's sustainability. In Matthew 6:33, when Jesus said:

"But seek first the kingdom of God and His righteousness, and all these things shall be added to you."

He expects our lives to be characterized by trust in Him for everything, a life of faith confidently expecting our daily bread. The attitude with which we obey is the defining factor in having our actions of service and sacrifice conform to the parameters of Kingdom behavior. Submission in the Kingdom means that we accept our Kingdom mandate with peace and joy. Romans 14:17 says:

...for the kingdom of God is not eating and drinking, but of righteousness and peace and joy in the Holy Spirit.

Thus, if we have no peace and no joy, we may not have entered the Kingdom. The entire basis of our Kingdom citizenry and our service to the King relies on our ability to scripturally submit to, not only the King, but to His reigning authorities on earth. Hebrews 13:17 tells us:

Obey those who rule over you, and be submissive, for they watch out for your souls, as those who must give account. Let them do so with joy and not with grief, for that would be unprofitable for you.

In the passage from Hebrews, the Greek word for "submit" is *hupotasso*, which is a verb that means "a voluntary attitude of giving in, cooperating, assuming responsibility, and carrying a burden." This word is originally a Greek military term meaning "to arrange [troop divisions] in a military fashion under the command of a leader". The scripture speaks clearly to our submission, as commanded by our spiritual covering who must give an account (ability) for us, because that is an advantage to us.

More important is the attitude with which we provide this sacrifice and service, which is the persevering mentality that says, "I will remain under". This mentality is the Greek work *hupomeno'*, or "I will persevere". It is to no advantage to a Kingdom citizen to be "double-minded." You cannot live in Christ's Kingdom with the keys to usher people in through evangelism and discipleship one day, and then the next day, rebel and say, "Hold these keys, I'll be right back – I gotta step outside into the other kingdom!" Initially, the act of submitting to your prophetic assignment is easy; it's exciting. But, in the Kingdom, the other parts of the Kingdom operating mentality will begin to come into play. Now you will be called on to die daily in order for the entire consulate or embassy to function. In the Kingdom, we must submit not only to our spiritual authorities, but to one another (same verb *hupotasso* is used in Ephesians 5:21) – as is true with our service. What does that mean? It means that we must "remain under" and persevere as we fight against our temperaments in dealing with one another on the earthly plane, as we are sanctified to fulfill our God-given purpose. It cannot matter that you grew up racist; it is immaterial to your spiritual purpose that you are more academically trained than another Kingdom citizen – God is not using your piety as a measuring stick against another Kingdom citizen who is less discipled! Our ability (or lack of ability) to see ourselves and others as God sees us cannot affect our attitude of joyful interaction. Consider Matthew 24:45-51:

> *"Who then is a faithful and wise servant, whom his master made ruler over his household, to give them food in due season? Blessed is that servant whom his master, when he comes, will find so doing. Assuredly, I say to you that he will make him ruler over all his goods. But if that evil servant says in his heart, 'My master is delaying his coming,' the master of that servant will come on a day when he is not looking for him and at an hour that he is not aware of, and begins to beat his fellow servants, and to eat and drink with the drunkards, and will cut him in two and appoint [him] his portion with the hypocrites. There shall be weeping and gnashing of teeth.*

We must strive not to be hypocrites; we must "remain under" and submit voluntarily to service and sacrifice with joy, because this is our mandate. Without the right attitude, submission is simply slavery – acting out of fear that is based on domination and control. Submission is manifested in attitudes and actions that align with the King. What makes this easier? Having the right DNA.

7. Sonship

Each of the Kingdom principles we've discussed have their foundation on one thing: sonship. This is very important, because the actual basis of the Kingdom is relationships, beginning with the relationship vertically with the Father and then the horizontal relationship we share with our spiritual family. If we have not successfully matriculated through our roles in life defined by sonship/daughterhood, brotherhood/sisterhood, manhood/womanhood and ultimately fatherhood/motherhood – and in that order, we have and will have issues. Therefore, the primary role into which we are all born and must successfully relate, before all others, is sonship (daughterhood) – first in the natural, then in the spirit (1 Corinthians 15:46).

When you give your life to Christ, you accept His Lordship and His heritage. Your lineage becomes established, even though you had been on earth for some time – the heir of your parents. Now you have divine parentage, which means several things. First, you are a new creation. In 2 Corinthians 5:17, scripture says:

> *Therefore, if anyone [is] in Christ, he is a new creation; old things have passed away; behold, all things have become new.*

God rules and reigns through your "new" man. Through Jesus, impartation of power is given to the second born; you should be governing your life through the spirit (your younger man).

161

Romans 9:8-12 states:

> *That is, those who [are] the children of the flesh, these [are] not the children of God; but the children of the promise are counted as the seed. For this is the word of promise: "At this time I will come and Sarah shall have a son." And not only [this], but when Rebecca also had conceived by one man, even by our father Isaac (for the children not yet being born, nor having done any good or evil, that the purpose of God according to election might stand, not of works but of Him who calls), it was said to her, "The older shall serve the younger."*

This is a very important concept to understand. When you give your life to Christ, you still have a chronological age and until then, you had been ruled by the whims, desires, and goals of your soul in accordance with the priorities of the world. At the moment you are reborn in Christ, you are a baby again, but you are God's baby. Now, your spirit man is younger than your soul man, and this new disciple under sanctification has to establish sonship by taking on the DNA of the Father who is in heaven. Why? So that God's purpose will stand. You are now part of another family, and those genetics must take precedence over all of the upbringing and ingraining that has gone on before in your life before salvation. Now, you are described in 1 Peter 2:9 as:

> *But you are a chosen generation, a royal priesthood, a holy nation, His own special people, that you may proclaim the praises of Him who called you out of darkness into His marvelous light.*

What are the three primary factors that define you now?

- Chosen Generation = *eklektos genos* = selected by God with His genes
- Royal Priesthood = *basileios hierateuma* = intercessors with kingly lineage
- Holy Nation = *hagios ethnos* = Gentiles (non-Jews) set aside by God to serve Him

Why? So that you may declare the praises of Him who called you. It's very difficult to submit, sacrifice, and serve if you do not have new DNA.

DNA has been called the fundamental building block of a person's entire genetic makeup. Your genus is now that of Christ; your calling is now administrated, developed, and fed through your spiritual shepherd. If you are not learning to hear the Kingdom and see the Kingdom so that you can understand your purpose in God's vision, then you are wasting your time 'going to church'. But if you have spent your life with a bad temper, low self-esteem, disrespecting women, using drugs...whatever the case may be, rebirth and sanctification can start shutting those practices down. You received a DNA transfusion at your rebirth, and as you consistently present your body to God, are properly shepherded, are transformed by the renewing your mind, and surrounded by others with the DNA of Christ, they will eventually go away.

You can expect to have a very difficult time converting your DNA if you have "daddy" issues, because you will first have to learn to see fatherhood correctly. How can you submit to being God's son, shepherded and parented spiritually by your pastor if you have spent your life rebelling against any paternal (or maternal, in some cases) authority? God's authority will feel like a choke chain! That's why being under instruction and meditating on the Word of God is so important in redefining your DNA. God, as your Father, cannot develop you into a man (or wo-man) of His, if you do open your mouth, chew your food, and swallow. The seed (Word) that is sown into you regularly is nourishment for the new creation you have become. Sonship requires that you understand some of the fundamentals of the temperament that you are acquiring, as well as identifying the temperament that you are attempting to shake off. The Kingdom temperament is the fruit of the Spirit and is defined in context in Galatians 5:19-26:

Now the works of the flesh are evident, which are: adultery, fornication, uncleanness, lewdness, idolatry, sorcery, hatred, contentions, jealousies, outbursts of wrath, selfish ambitions, dissensions, heresies, envy, murders, drunkenness, revelries, and the like; of which I tell you beforehand, just as I also told you in time past, that those who practice such things will not inherit the kingdom of God. But the fruit of the Spirit is love, joy, peace, longsuffering, kindness, goodness, faithfulness, gentleness, self-control. Against such there is no law. And those who are Christ's have crucified the flesh with its passions and desires. If we live in the Spirit, let us also walk in the Spirit. Let us not become conceited, provoking one another, envying one another..

Your new DNA should be manifesting all of these positive attributes simultaneously. Many people are deceived by the term "fruit"; fruit is not plural. Think of it like an orange with many sections – it is one fruit! The Holy Spirit is the Third Person of the Trinity who keeps us, lives in us, works through us, and cultivates the growth of His fruit in your life. We cannot work in our own might on any one part of the fruit; this is spiritual-seeded and cultivated fruit. Galatians 5: 17 instructs us that the fruit of the Spirit will manifest as we walk in the Spirit.

Sonship is the core of our connection with all Kingdom citizens. We have to remember that we are part of a nation of sons of God; thus, after sonship, we experience brotherhood/sisterhood. We are relational with each other in the Kingdom, and we constantly recognize that a work is being done in all of us individually and collectively. Think about it in the natural. Usually, no matter how far you fall out with a sibling – there's a bond that cannot be broken – it's in your blood. In the Kingdom, we should prize this shared blood of Christ, because we share royal blood, election, and holiness.

Protecting this relationship amongst ourselves is what keeps the Kingdom of God strong; violating these bonds based on man-made divisions of race, class, and other societal delineations is what has made the Christian church weak.

These are the seven drivers or building blocks of a Kingdom mentality that every Kingdom citizen must possess. The Kingdom of God is internally consistent. Each and every one of these principles we have discussed is interdependent. God is sovereign, thus we serve Him. You cannot be a good servant and not observe structure; you cannot observe structure and not sacrifice; you cannot serve unless you submit, you cannot render the proper service and sacrifice for God's purposes, if you're not a Son. This is a package. Study these drivers and then apply them to your personal life as a Kingdom citizen. As you can see, being a Kingdom citizen represents much more than being a church member.

Chapter Eight:
The Seven Drivers in Operation

This chapter is designed to assist the Kingdom citizen in further understanding the building blocks of the Kingdom – the seven drivers. These drivers will provide you with the content of thinking or the development of a Kingdom mentality. We will examine the basic tenets of the seven drivers and then I have provided exercises to help you store them in your spirit and mind, so that you can operate with a Kingdom mentality everyday.

Kingdom Sovereignty

Components of Sovereignty

ABSOLUTE POWER

Power is one of the components that contribute to the state of sovereignty. But exactly what is power? In science, power is defined as "the ability to do work". However, in the area of human relationships and interactions, power is defined as "the ability to influence the actions of others or to control the environment around oneself." Thus, by combining these two definitions, we arrive at a working definition of power as "the ability to make things happen and/or get things done!"

AUTONOMY

The second component of sovereignty is autonomy. This word refers to self-sufficiency and can be defined in numerous ways depending upon the discipline in question.

AUTHORITY

The third component of sovereignty is authority. Although most people think of power and authority as being synonymous, there is quite a bit of difference in the meanings and implications of these words. While power refers to a person's ability to act, authority is best defined as "a person's right to act."

Authority refers to the extent to which a person has been duly vested and officially sanctioned to use power. Authority answers the question of whether a person's power is legitimate or not. For example, while a teen-aged baby-sitter might have the power (ability) to spank your child, parents who do not believe in corporal punishment would argue that the sitter does not have the authority (right) to do so.

Man's Response to the Sovereign God

How should man respond to the sovereignty of God? Within the scriptures, we find three examples that provide us insight to this question for the modern believer. After encountering the Lord of hosts in chapter 6, the prophet Isaiah recognized his state. He experienced:

Conviction: "Woe is me, for I am undone!" (v.5)

When Isaiah entered the presence of the Lord, he was immediately compelled to admit the truth about himself in comparison to a perfect God. When a person really meets God, there is an immediate recognition of sinful nature.

Confession: "Because I am a man of unclean lips, and I dwell in the midst of a people of unclean lips; for my eyes have seen the King, the LORD of hosts." (v.5)

In the light of God's perfection, Isaiah saw himself, and of his own volition, confessed and repented. Job had a similar encounter and reaction after he was interrogated by God.

"Behold, I am vile; What shall I answer You? I lay my hand over my mouth. – Job 40:4

Then Job answered the LORD and said: "I know that You can do everything, and that no purpose of Yours can be withheld from You. You asked, 'Who is this who hides counsel without knowledge?' Therefore I have uttered what I did not understand, things too wonderful for me, which I did not know. Listen, please, and let me speak; You said, 'I will question you, and you shall answer Me.' "I have heard of You by the hearing of the ear, but now my eye sees You. Therefore I abhor myself, and repent in dust and ashes." – Job 42:1-6

Job recognized his imperfect condition compared to the sovereign God, humbled himself, as the prophet Isaiah did, and repented of his former pride and arrogance by refusing to speak any further.

Conversion: Then one of the seraphim flew to me, having in his hand a live coal which he had taken with the tongs from the altar. And he touched my mouth with it, and said: "Behold, this has touched your lips; your iniquity is taken away, and your sin purged." (vv.6-7)

Once Isaiah confessed then repented, the supernatural conversion of His spirit took place. Godly conviction that does not lead to confession and repentance is called remorse, and it does not lead to conversion.

Challenge: Also I heard the voice of the Lord, saying: Whom shall I send, and who will go for Us? Then I said, "Here am I! Send me!" (v.8)

And the Lord restored Job's losses when he prayed for his friends. Indeed the Lord gave Job twice as much as he had before. – Job 42:10

The appropriate response to the sovereign Lord and King is submission to His will. Isaiah and Job's experience with God compelled them to obey God and submit themselves to the purpose for which He chose them.

Sovereignty and Divine Attributes

Sovereignty is a divine attribute of God alone. Other divine attributes include:

- Autonomous – Isaiah 46:9-11, 2 Corinthians 3:17
- Omnipotent – Jeremiah 32:17, Matthew 19:26
- Omnipresent – Psalm 139:7-12
- Omniscient – 1 John 3:20, Job 37:16
- Perfect – Deuteronomy 32:4, Matthew 5:48
- Just – Psalm 89:14; 97:2
- Holy – Isaiah 43:3
- Love – 1 John 4:8

Summary

The first driver of the Kingdom is sovereignty. In the Kingdom of God, God is sovereign. By definition, He has "the exclusive right to exercise absolute authority, power, and dominion over a geographic region or group of people without interference or intrusion from any outside force or entity". The five components of sovereignty are absolute power, autonomy, authority, knowledge, and understanding. As believers, God is our sovereign master, thus He has ownership over all things, authority to enforce His will upon all creation, and complete control over the universe.

The appropriate response to the sovereign Lord is conviction, confession, and challenge after conversion. The first three speak to the salvific experience that all believers have experienced. The fourth, however, speaks to the believer's desire to obey God irrespective of contradicting plans, desires, and emotions.

Whatever stops us from following the King's instructions is the thing that drives us more than the sovereignty of God, and this should not be so.

Whether it is personal comfort, fear of social rejection, resistance to change, or fear of failure that stops us, we serve the autonomous, omnipotent, omnipresent, omniscient, perfect, just, holy and loving King. This week, demonstrate the sovereignty of God and execute the orders of the King.

What has the sovereign King instructed you to do that you have neglected to wholeheartedly accomplish? (Remember He has commanded us all to make disciples.)

In the space provided below, make a list of the things that stop you from executing Christ's instructions with zeal.

_____

_____

_____

_____

_____

_____

_____

_____

_____

_____

_____

_____

_____

Kingdom Stewardship

Our discussion of stewardship has taught us that God requires us to be good stewards. God created and owns everything. So, Kingdom believers must learn to effectively manage what God entrusts to us. What does stewardship include – everything. What does it exclude – nothing. So, Kingdom believers must relate to all that we have as those who must give it back and report what we did with it – a serious responsibility with serious repercussions.

Jesus stated emphatically that no man can serve two masters. Stewardship is the one area that will allow you to examine and concretely determine whether God or money rules your life. To understand stewardship, you must first understand the servant/ master relationship in the Kingdom, as taught by Jesus in Matthew 25.

Tithing and the Old Testament
In the Garden of Eden, God told Adam that the fruit of the Tree of the Knowledge of Good and Evil should not be eaten. Even though he could enjoy all that God provided in the Garden, the fruit of that tree could not be eaten. We know that God does not eat fruit, so the tree was in the Garden of Eden to establish the following principle: No matter how much I give to you, you must understand that a portion of everything I give to you belongs to Me. Thus, God establishes this principle of consecration in the very first book of scripture. Other Old Testament examples of tithing include (Leviticus 27:30):

- The annual tithe for the Priest – Leviticus 27:30-32, Numbers 18:21-24
- The annual tithe for the Feast – Deuteronomy 12:17-18
- The benevolence tithe (every third year) – Deuteronomy 14:28-29; 26:12-15

Pre-Law Stewardship
- Adam – Genesis 2:15
- Cain – Genesis 4
- Abel – Genesis 4
- Jacob (10%) – Genesis 28
- Abram – Genesis 14
- The Exodus – Exodus 4:23

Offerings

Five is the number of grace; scripture outlines five offerings that could be made to God:

1. Burnt offerings
2. Grain offerings
3. Peace offerings
4. Sin offerings
5. Guilt offerings

Christ and Stewardship

Christ inaugurated the message of the Kingdom of God and with it, an emphasis on spiritual existence in the earth realm. Christ constantly taught on giving and the necessity of allowing God to transform the way people felt about and related to money and possessions. The Bible states that you cannot serve two masters – your service to one immediately results in the rejection of the other. While many believers give their hearts to Christ and confess Him as Lord, their focus never changes in terms of what they seek after in life! Unfortunately, they still desire and pursue the same earthly treasures they sought after prior to their conversion. Regarding this trend, the Apostle Paul admonishes:

> If then you were raised with Christ, seek those things which are above, where Christ is, sitting at the right hand of God. Set your mind on things above, not on things on the earth. For you died, and your life is hidden with Christ in God. – Colossians 3:1-3

Our focus and energy on getting wealth should pale in comparison to the focus and energy we place on seeking the Kingdom. Jesus teaches us the proper response to finding the Kingdom in two powerful parables: The Parable of the Hidden Treasure and the Parable of the Pearl of Great Price (Matthew 13:44-46).

God owns everything that we have, and we own absolutely nothing! This is one of the principles that is diametrically opposed to what we have been taught prior to entering the Kingdom. God expects your time, energy, relationships, homes, transportation, gifts and talents… everything that He has placed in your life to be under your Kingdom stewardship and used to fulfill His will that will glorify Him.

Tithing and the New Testament

Tithing did not begin with the law, and consequently, it is not affected by the fulfillment of the law and the coming of Christ. Thus, when Jesus addressed the Pharisees, He acknowledged their obedience to the tithe.

> Woe to you, scribes and Pharisees, hypocrites! For you pay tithe of mint and anise and cummin, and have neglected the weightier matters of the law: justice and mercy and faith. These you ought to have done, without leaving the others undone. – Matthew 23:23

Clearly, Jesus endorsed tithing, and as such, believers are required to live by and honor this expectation.

Ten Wisdom Principles of Stewardship

With the tithe, the Bible specifically requires Kingdom citizens to bring a set amount to God. However, there are no such parameters in scripture for the offering. However, the Bible provides us principles regarding the offering that help us give to God and demonstrate our faith in Him.

1. God loves a cheerful giver – 2 Corinthians 9:6-8
2. Give willingly in specific offerings – Exodus 25:1-9
3. Put God first in giving offerings – Proverbs 3:9 -10
4. Give God your best offerings, and He will accept them – Genesis 4:3-5
5. Give in times of poverty and in times of abundance – Luke 21:1-4
6. Consider the poor and give – Leviticus 19:10, Deuteronomy 24:21-22
7. Giving has benefits – Luke 6:38, Galatians 6:6-10, 2 Corinthians 9:6
8. You will increase in your intimacy with God – Matthew 6:21
9. Giving is an investment for eternity – Matthew 6:19-20
10. When blessed, continue giving, be humble, trust God – 1 Timothy 6:17-19

A process exists that can help you as a believer see everything in your life as God's and available for His use. The Holy Spirit will teach you throughout your sanctification process. However, the process of stewardship begins with:

- Giving yourself first to Christ – 2 Corinthians 8:5
- Submitting yourself to spiritual leadership – Philippians 4:15-20
- Embracing the vision of the local church – Acts 4:34-35
- Seeking the Kingdom with priority – Matthew 6:33

Summary

In order to faithfully live the life of a steward, believers must understand the intent and uses of money, time, skills, people, and material things in order to remain under the umbrella of His favor and blessings. The Word of God demands that believers choose between serving the master of the natural world, money, and seeking the Kingdom of God.

Christ encourages believers by stating that if they seek the Kingdom of God and the righteousness of Christ the King, all of their earthly needs will be provided for. This is true only to the extent that believers realize that all that they possess belongs to God and has been entrusted to their care by His grace. Those driven by the stewardship driver view the resources that they have access to, not their own, but the King's. Thus, they manage these resources in such a way as to please the King.

The rest of your life can dramatically change with a sincere commitment to tithe and give offerings. Answer the questions below and pray for obedience and a steward's spirit toward all that God has placed in your care.

Are you a consistent tither? ❑ Yes ❑ No

Will you commit to tithing before any bills are paid to ensure your consistency? ❑ Yes ❑ No

How any hours per month will you commit to ministry service? _____ hrs

What is your monthly offering goal? $_____

Who, in your ministry's leadership, will you share these goals with, asking them to keep you accountable?

Name:_____

Kingdom Structure

God is the God of order. He took a world that was void and without form, arranged it perfectly, gave it order, and then delegated a representative and a helper to oversee it. Thus, everything in the Kingdom of God is governed by structure. God established structure in the Kingdom and expects everything under His sovereign rule to operate within it.

Apostolic Order

The apostolic refers to representatives sent on behalf of the Kingdom and can be described as God's established government in action. The church describes those who have been called out and set aside to establish God's rule and reign on the earth. The apostolic establishes the embassy in:

- **Development** (1 Corinthians 3:9-11) – The pastor is God's co-laborer. The church body is God's field. The pastor oversees us for maximum productivity.
- **Doctrine** (Acts 2:42) – The collection of beliefs and principles that set up the parameters of faith of believers in Jesus Christ.
- **Discipleship** (2 Corinthians 5:20) – The culture of the church that reflects the purpose for which every believer has been called and chosen by God (The Great Commission). Discipleship/fruitfulness is one of the necessary signs of being a disciple of Christ (John 15:1-8).
- **Direction** (Acts 4:35-5:2) – The five-fold ministry office leads – you follow. Jesus, on several occasions, compared men and women to sheep who needed a shepherd to lead them where they needed to go.
- **Discipline** (2 Thessalonians 5:12, Hebrews 13:7, 17) – The five-fold ministry offices have rule over you. This rule is based upon the authority of scripture. In turn, officers of the church must govern according to scripture and refrain from the abuse of authority.

The church is the property of God and was intended to be a powerful and mighty force on this earth for the saving of souls. The church was created to be a reflection of Christ's Kingdom and literally serves as its embassy.

Structure and Five-fold Ministry (Ephesians 4:11-12)	• Apostles • Prophets • Evangelists • Pastors • Teachers
Structure and the Apostolic (1 Corinthians 12:28)	• Apostles • Prophets • Teachers • Miracles • Gifts of healings • Helps • Administrations • Tongues
Structure and Apostolic Order	• Christ is the head of the church – Ephesians 1:22, Colossians 1:18 • Christ is the head of man – 1 Corinthians 11:1-3 • Husband is the head of household – Colossians 3:18-23, Ephesians 5:22-31 • Wives • Children • Servants

Summary

Structure is the second driver of the Kingdom. Throughout scripture and creation, God uses the number 12 – the number of government – to establish structure and order. A king uses structure or government to establish and maintain order within the borders of his kingdom. Government was God's idea; Jesus established the church as His organization of post-resurrection apostolic order. Jesus commissioned the five-fold ministry gifts of apostles, prophets, evangelists, pastors, and teachers to establish structure in His church. Order in Kingdom families contribute to the order of the Kingdom and allows the church and work of God to grow immensely in width and breadth, forever remaining viable and productive.

Everyone in the Kingdom of God is governed by His structure, so to ignore Kingdom structure is an indication that you have not entered His Kingdom. His structure requires that we esteem the offices of apostle, prophet, evangelist, pastor and teacher, which lead us, as representatives of Him. They are your shepherds. In addition, the apostolic structure they construct (those to whom they have delegated authority) should be respected and honored.

A believer who is driven by the Kingdom driver of structure looks to their leader's direction as their message from God and submits in faith. Do you have a leader? Do you use your leader's preached message as God's direction for your life?

In the space below, list the directions God has given you through your leader's last sermon (or meeting with you). If you can't remember them, purchase the CD of the message.

_____

_____

_____

_____

Create a plan to implement every aspect of your leader's message, considering the items above. Ask yourself:

Am I implementing this? ❑ Yes ❑ No

How will I implement it?

_____

_____

_____

_____

_____

_____

_____

What is stopping me from implementation?

_____

_____

_____

_____

_____

_____

When will I implement it?
Date: _____

Kingdom Servanthood

You're saved! Now what? Good question! Your confession of Christ as Lord has just launched you into a world of opposites – the Kingdom of God. In God's Kingdom, greatness is obtained through servanthood! Service is one of the key, defining characteristics of the life of the Kingdom citizen. How should we serve? Who should we serve? Let's examine the fifth driver of the Kingdom in review and find out.

Christ's Service – Service Through Revelation

Jesus said to them, "My food is to do the will of Him who sent Me, and to finish His work. – John 4:34

"For I have come down from heaven, not to do My own will, but the will of Him who sent Me. This is the will of the Father who sent Me, that of all He has given Me I should lose nothing, but should raise it up at the last day. And this is the will of Him who sent Me, that everyone who sees the Son and believes in Him may have everlasting life; and I will raise him up at the last day. – John 6:38-40

Christ served man by revealing the will of God the Father. According to John 1:1 and 1:14, Christ is God; He was the Word of God, manifested in human flesh among men. His purpose was to reveal the nature, person, and ways of God in the world in a manner that could be received and desired.

Christ's Service – Service Through Reconciliation

Christ served mankind by revealing and executing the plan of His Father; that plan was the salvation of all those who recognize, confess, and believe in the Lordship of Christ.

"...for the Son of Man has come to seek and to save that which was lost." – Luke 19:10

Jesus' reference to seeking and saving "that which was lost" is, in part, a reference to the Jewish community of which He said, 'I was not sent except to the lost sheep of the house of Israel' (Matthew 15:24). Yet, the Jews did not receive and believe in Jesus, and salvation was made available, according to the Apostle Paul, to those who were "afar off" (Acts 2:39), a reference to the Gentile community who constituted the entire rest of the world. Though it seems that salvation of the Gentiles was an afterthought, God in His omniscience, knew the Jews would not accept Jesus and had already made a provision for non-Jewish people (Romans 9:23-26).

One of our working definitions of a servant is one who does not consider his own agenda. Regardless of the rejection He received at the hands of man, Jesus' assignment was to provide the means for man to be restored into right relationship with God. He was faithful to this end unto death. He attended to the needs of the lost by living a sinless and perfect life; a life whose sacrifice satisfied the righteous requirement of God. His service resulted in the availability of salvation through reconciliation to all mankind.

The Believer's Preparation for Service

As believers in the Kingdom of God, we are called to pattern our lives after the life of Christ. We are called to serve! However, we cannot simply 'get saved' one day and begin serving the next. The service we are called to execute has eternal consequences. Therefore, we must be properly prepared before we begin. Our preparation for service takes place in a three-step process.

Step 1: Studying

In the gospels, Christ details the first step believers should take before being sent out to serve. In Matthew 11:28-30, He extends a call and gives a command by stating:

"Come to Me, all you who labor and are heavy laden, and I will give you rest. Take My yoke upon you and learn from Me, for I am gentle and lowly in heart, and you will find rest for your souls. For My yoke is easy and My burden is light.

These passages of scripture are symbolic of the call of salvation God extends to all mankind through Christ. Jesus encourages humanity to come and find rest in Him – this rest is the equivalent of man's salvation experience. Next, Christ commands us to "take My yoke... and learn from Me". With this line, Christ calls the believer to study.

Study is defined as "the pursuit of knowledge by reading, observation, research, or attentive scrutiny". Thus, before we begin to serve in the Kingdom of God, we are expected to devote ourselves to learn the Word of God in order to know the manner in which we are to serve and the ways in which our service is to be carried out. The proper procedure for this process was displayed in the life of Paul.

Step 2: Continuing

Defined as "persisting or going on with a particular action or in a particular condition", the second step in the believer's preparation for service is continuing! Remember, Jesus is our model for service – His life is the paradigm after which our lives are to be patterned. In John 8:31a, He tells His followers:

"If you abide (continue) in My word, you are My disciples indeed.

This sentiment was echoed by the Apostle Paul who instructed Timothy to also continue in the Word of God. He writes:

Take heed to yourself and to the doctrine. Continue in them, for in doing this you will save both yourself and those who hear you. – 1 Timothy 4:16

But you must continue in the things which you have learned and been assured of, knowing from whom you have learned them… – 2 Timothy 3:14

Both scriptures emphasize the first and second steps involved in the believer's preparation for service: study and continuing! Paul intended to encourage Timothy to remain focused on doctrine, teaching, and instruction, which were the basis of his ministry. By constantly taking heed of the things he learned as Paul's pupil and faithfully practicing all he learned at the apostle's feet, Timothy was sure to be the voice of salvation for those who embraced his teachings. As believers, we must appropriate Paul's instructions to Timothy and apply them to our personal walks with God. In order to be properly prepared to serve in God's Kingdom, we must continue in His Word.

Step 3: Standing

Finally, my brethren, be strong in the Lord and in the power of His might. Put on the whole armor of God, that you may be able to stand against the wiles of the devil. For we do not wrestle against flesh and blood, but against principalities, against powers, against the rulers of the darkness of this age, against spiritual hosts of wickedness in the heavenly places. Therefore take up the whole armor of God, that you may be able to withstand in the evil day, and having done all, to stand. Stand therefore… – Ephesians 6:10-14a

In Paul's letter to the Ephesians, Paul warned the believers to prepare for service by becoming devil-ready. He encouraged them to stand and then stand beyond the point of quitting. Paul does not speak as if Satan might attack. Instead, He spoke with the surety and confidence of a man who had experienced Satan's attacks and knew what was needed to prepare for, stand against, and rebuff him. Thus, this is the last step in the believer's three-step process of preparation for Kingdom service.

Kingdom Servants

- Servants of the King – John 12:26
- Servants are one of the greatest in the Kingdom – Mark 10:43
- Servants serve the King – Matthew 22:13
- Servants are chosen – Matthew 22:14

Servanthood Defined

The different types of servants:

διάκονος (*diakonos*) –

1. generally of a person who renders helpful service, servant, helper (Matthew 20:26, Romans 16:1)
2. as an official in the church; deacon, both masculine (1 Timothy 3:8) and feminine (Romans 16:1)
3. as a government official minister, agent (Romans 13:4)
4. as one who serves a high official attendant, servant (Matthew 22:13)

The Kingdom Servant

- Attitude – John 12:25-26
- Aspirations – Colossians 3:1-3, Matthew 6:33
- Actions – Mark 10:43-44

The Seven Interrogatives of Kingdom Service

1. When do we serve?
2. Where do we serve?
3. Why do we serve?
4. Who do we serve?
5. How do we serve?
6. What do we serve (provide)?
7. Unto whom do we serve?

The Call to Serve Christ

Kingdom Assignment (Luke 14:15-24)

- Invite
- Bring
- Compel

In the Kingdom of God, we serve the King and His purpose when we:

- Evangelize – Acts 1:8
- Expose Satan – Acts 26:18
- Explain the consequences of sin – Romans 3:23; 6:23
- Express God's love – John 3:16, Romans 5:8, 1 John 4:7-11
- Allow entrance to the Kingdom – Matthew 16:19
- Educate – 2 Timothy 2:2, Matthew 28:20
- Encourage spiritual discipline and maturity – Galatians 6:1, Hebrews 6:1
- Exalt the King – Matthew 5:16

The scriptures provide additional reasons why we should willingly commit our lives to serving God:

- Friendship (John 15:15)
- Inheritance
- Reward (Colossians 3:24, Revelation 22:12)

Summary

Salvation is not the end toward which men's lives should aspire. Rather, it is the first step in a life that is to be lived in service to and in the Kingdom of God. We are Kingdom servants, and at His behest, we serve. As believers, we are called to follow Jesus' example of service and serve the needs of both sinners and saints alike. However, before our ministry of service can begin, we must be properly prepared and equipped to serve. Our service is to be offered with joy – understanding the grace given to us to serve – and filled with gratitude at the opportunity to be called a friend of God.

As Kingdom citizens, we serve the King by representing Him to those who don't know Him. In the space provided below, list seven unsaved people you know. Pray for the salvation of those on your list.

1. _____

2. _____

3. _____

4. _____

5. _____

6. _____

7. _____

Remember that a Kingdom servant has to have the right:

- Attitude – John 12:25-26
- Aspirations – Colossians 3:1-3, Matthew 6:33
- Actions – Mark 10:43-44

In the space provided below, list intentional efforts that you will make to represent Christ to each person listed above.

1. _____

2. _____

3. _____

4. _____

5. _____

6. _____

7. _____

Kingdom Sacrifice

Life in the Kingdom of God demands prioritization of God's goals and desires at the expense of our personal goals, ambitions, and desires. Thus, sacrifice is perhaps one of the most difficult principles to master. Prescribed by God, rooted in the practices of the Old Testament Levitical priests, and central to the message of the Kingdom of God, sacrifice is a Kingdom driver and mindset that must be embraced by all who desire to live successful lives in the Kingdom of God. Closely related to servanthood in acts and behaviors of service, sacrifice, delves deeper into God's requirement for Kingdom believers.

Sacrifice Defined

Well, let's begin our discussion of sacrifice by defining the term. In the spirit realm, sacrifice is defined as "the religious practice of offering food, objects (typically valuables), or the lives of animals or people to the gods as an act of propitiation or worship". It can also be defined as "giving up something of your own, especially for someone else." Generally, if you were to ask any person who claimed to be a follower of Christ to describe sacrifice, they would likely do so in these terms – making reference to the act of giving something up for the benefit of someone else. However, they would be in error.

The Believer's Lifestyle of Sacrifice

Jesus sacrificed His life that all humanity might have the opportunity to enjoy a loving and intimate relationship with God the Father. Believers are the beneficiaries of His sacrifice. However, we are not simply called to enjoy the benefits of His death and live freely without responsibilities or expectations. Just as Christ's death was not an end in and of itself – but a means to an end, the sinner's salvation must be regarded and approached in the same manner. Just as Christ died for a specific purpose and cause, we now live, having been reborn in and of the Spirit for that very purpose and cause.

This purpose is only achieved when we follow the example of Christ and offer our lives to God. This offering is the beginning of the believer's lifestyle of sacrifice.

The Call to Death

In his work *The Cost of Discipleship*, German theologian Dietrich Bonhoeffer writes "When Christ calls a man, he bids him come and die…". This call to death is the challenge every believer is faced with following His confession of Christ as Lord. Bonhoeffer's reference to the call of Christ is likely derived from the invitation from Christ to the lost in Mark 8:34b. He said:

> *"Whoever desires to come after Me, let him deny himself, and take up his cross, and follow Me.*

In Mark 8:34, Christ stated, without apology, that in order to successfully follow Him, you must first die. The cross is the ultimate symbol of self-sacrifice and, just as Jesus' death was attained through the cross, each believer must choose to die to himself, "take up his cross" for someone else, and fulfill the will of God for his life. Both self-denial and self-crucifixion refer to death of one's self for the benefit of another.

From Death to Life to Death?

We came to God spiritually dead, having experienced eternal separation from Him. Concerning our former state, Paul writes that as sinners, we were once dead in trespasses:

> *But God, who is rich in mercy, because of His great love with which He loved us, even when we were dead in trespasses, made us alive together with Christ (by grace you have been saved), and raised us up together, and made us sit together in the heavenly places in Christ Jesus… – Ephesians 2:4-6*

By virtue of our natural birth, we were sinners – we possessed the genetic sin-stain of Adam and, as a result, deserved death. However, just as in the Garden, through the richness of His grace, God provided a means for us to escape the penalty of death through our confession and belief in Christ who died on our behalf. Thus, our confession accomplished the following:

- Our spirit man was made alive
- We died to ourselves
- We were seated with Christ in heavenly places
- We were left on earth to continue Christ's work
- We live with a Christ-focused agenda

So through our new birth, we were made to be alive in Christ. But now are we supposed to die again?

Death of self-will and self-benefiting circumstances is the only way that we can progress in the Kingdom of God. After we receive life in Jesus Christ, we have the daunting task of imitating Him in our lives. Through the Holy Spirit, God takes us through careful chastening to transform us into the image of His Son and prepare us for our call. This process is called sanctification by grace. But God, ever mindful of our free will, does not force us to be His sons, obey His precepts, and submit to His call. Paul instructs that we must do that ourselves:

I beseech you therefore, brethren, by the mercies of God, that you present your bodies a living sacrifice, holy, acceptable to God, which is your reasonable service. – Romans 12:1

The Three Courts of the Tabernacle
- The Outer Court
- The Inner Court or Holy Place
- The Holy of Holies

The Tabernacle and Sacrifice
- The Furniture of the Tabernacle
- The Brazen Altar
- Laver
- Table of Shewbread
- Altar of Incense
- Candlesticks
- Ark of the Covenant

The Attitude of Sacrifice – New Testament Priesthood
- Presentation – Romans 12:1
- Praise – Hebrews 13:15, 1 Peter 2:9
- Prioritized sowing – Philippians 4:15-19

Return on Investment of Sacrifice
- Abundant Life – John 10:10
- Propitiation – 1 John 2:2
- Justification – Romans 8:30
- Reconciliation – Romans 5:11
- Regeneration – Titus 3:5
- Eternal Life – John 3:16

Summary

Believers in the Kingdom of God are called to a lifestyle of self-sacrifice. This sacrifice calls for the wishes and mandates of the King to be prioritized over our own desires. We must follow the model of Christ who demonstrates the highest degree of sacrifice available to man – the sacrifice of His life that others might live. As we strive toward this end, God promises to reward us and add the things we will need on our journey to fulfill His purpose.

With the list of unsaved people you created in Kingdom Servanthood, use the space below and write out your strategy to present the gospel and disciple them.

How many hours a week will you sacrifice for this? (Don't attempt to approach all seven people on your list at once; approach each one at a time.)

_____ hrs

In your strategy, include:

- A plan to fellowship with them
- Other believers that you want to help you build relationships with the potential disciple
- Set times to pray for them

_____

_____

_____

_____

_____

_____

_____

_____

_____

_____

_____

_____

_____

_____

Kingdom Submission

Submission is often seen as a negative term of subordination or inferiority. However, Kingdom submission, as outlined in the Bible, is vital in the life of Kingdom citizens. Jesus Himself submitted to the will of the Father in the Garden of Gethsemane when he stated:

...nevertheless, not My will, but Yours, be done." – Luke 22:42

Submission Defined
Defined in the natural as "the act of yielding or surrendering to another of higher authority", submission is the third driver of the Kingdom of God. In the most basic terms, the Kingdom of God can be defined as "the rule or reign of God in the hearts of men." We have already established that God is the self-sufficient, sovereign Lord of all creation who rules and reigns in autonomy, knowledge, wisdom, omnipotence, and authority through an established structure. Based upon this understanding of God, we are called to exist in full submission to His will and His structure and to understand the necessity of adhering to His commands as subjects of His Kingdom.

Submission is the voluntary attitude of giving in, cooperating, assuming responsibility, and carrying a burden. Taken together, submission to the King means to voluntarily give into the reign, rule, and will of the all-powerful, all-knowing, self-sufficient God. The attitude with which we obey is the defining factor that must be present for our actions of service and sacrifice to conform to the parameters of Kingdom behavior. Submission in the Kingdom of God means that we accept our Kingdom assignment and carry it out with joy.

To Whom Are We Called to Submit?
Clearly, submission was intended by God to be a part of the believer's life in the Kingdom. The scriptures explicitly detail and outline the conditions under which we are called to submit.

The Bible is the voice of God Himself, and it carries just as much weight as God speaking to us face to face. Thus, believers are called to submit to the Word of God. The Word of God provides the guidance and direction we need to discover and fulfill God's will for your life.

Your word is a lamp to my feet and a light to my path. – Psalm 119:105

Submitting to the Word entails not only quoting it, but consistent application of the Word in daily living. In order to do this, one has to trust and believe that the scriptures are the final authority on a relationship with God. We believe that the Bible is inerrant, perfectly inspired, and compiled by God. Paul states:

All Scripture is given by inspiration of God, and is profitable for doctrine, for reproof, for correction, for instruction in righteousness: that the man of God may be complete, thoroughly equipped for every good work. – 2 Timothy 3:16-17

The Word of God reveals the mind of God, and as such, must be the final authority in the life of the believer.

Submission and Watchmen

The responsibility of God's watchmen is to preach the Word of God without compromise or care regarding the people's response. The responsibility of the people of God is to receive the Word of God, apply it to our lives, and live according to its commands. Believers should never lose sight of the fact that in the relationship between the watchman and those under his care, the greatest level of weight and responsibility lies with the watchman. He has been commissioned by God to feed God's people with knowledge and understanding (Jeremiah 3:15), to watch for their souls (Ezekiel 33:4), and to give an account (Hebrews 13:17).

Submission and the Family (Husbands, Wives, and Children)

> *But I want you to know that the head of every man is Christ, the head of woman is man, and the head of Christ is God. – 1 Corinthians 11:3*

Although men and women have equal access to God through their relationship with Christ, the scriptures define specific roles each must fulfill in the marital relationship. The husband is to assume leadership in the home (1 Corinthians 11:3, Ephesians 5:23). This leadership should not be dictatorial, condescending, or patronizing to the wife, but should be in accordance with the example of Christ leading the church (servant/leader).

It is the design of God to submit to His Word through assigned delegates, what is called apostolic order. Paul argues apostolic order in 1 Corinthians 11:1-16. He speaks of how God governs His Kingdom through divine order and suggests that submission to God is submission to His Word through His selected form of leadership. However, we are not to submit simply to offices and genders, but to the Word of God. Hence, if a person is in the role of leadership and is clearly violating the Word of God, we are not called to submit to the will of man, but the Word of God!

> *If then you were raised with Christ, seek those things which are above, where Christ is, sitting at the right hand of God. Set your mind on things above, not on things on the earth. For you died, and your life is hidden with Christ in God. – Colossians 3:1-3*

Benefits of Submission
The scriptures detail some very real benefits that are available as a result of humbling oneself under the rule and reign of the King and those whom He places in positions of authority.

- Sanctuary – Psalm 91:1-71
- Salvation – Psalm 50:22-23
- Security – James 4:6-8
- Sensitivity – John 9:31
- Exaltation – 1 Peter 5:6

Summary

As citizens of the Kingdom, we are called to submit to the finished work of Christ, who instituted a more excellent way to serve and honor God. Defined in the natural as "the act of yielding or surrendering to another of higher authority." Submission means to remain under. As believers, we are called to exist in full submission to God's will and to understand the necessity of adhering to His commands as subjects of His Kingdom. We willfully surrender our desires, ambitions, and ourselves to service for the King.

Submission is not simply about obedience; He wants us to serve Him from our hearts. Every Kingdom citizen should submit in attitude and behavior to the Word of God and to God's watchmen. The benefits of submission are safekeeping, salvation, security, a harmonious relationship with God, and promotion from the Lord. For there to be submission, there must first be disagreement. When two agree, they cooperate; however when they disagree, one has the opportunity to yield to the other. Submission can then take place. Thus, how we manage conflict with those in authority is critical to this driver.

We are called to submit to the Word of God, which outlines obedience to His structures in the world, the church, and in the family.

Think back to that last time you disagreed with the Word or God's structure. How did you react?

_____

_____

_____

_____

_____

_____

Remember, submission is not simply about obedience; He wants us to serve Him from our hearts. Did you model submission in the situation above? If not, reread and memorize the appropriate scriptures previously given. How should you have reacted?

_____

_____

_____

_____

_____

Use the scriptures that you memorized to help you yield the next time a similar situation arises.

Kingdom Sonship

Children are the pride of their fathers, the objects of adoration of their mothers, and signify the relationship that exists between God and those who have confessed Christ as Lord, recognize His sovereignty, honor His order and specific design for all creation, and submit their lives to His will.

Positional and Conditional Sonship
The second letter to the Corinthians, chapter five, verse 17 says that if anyone is in Christ, he is a new creation; old things have passed away; behold, all things have become new. The Apostle Paul was trying to explain the spiritual transformation that occurs when one enters the Kingdom of God, by the Spirit of God, through the Word of God. However, just as all the potential that exists in the natural parent-child relationship cannot and is not experienced upon the birth of a child, the fullness of spiritual sonship is not experienced as a result of simply being born again. Something more is required.

For as many as are led by the Spirit of God, these are sons of God. – Romans 8:14

In his letter to the church at Rome, Paul asserts that sonship and the title of son are not conferred upon men and women who simply receive and accept Christ and His Kingdom message. Though they occupy the position of son, this title and role does not refer to a static state of existence. Indeed, Paul states that the word "sons" is the term by which those who, after their confession of Christ, exemplify a true father-son relationship by submitting to the leadership of the Father and allowing themselves to be led and directed by the Holy Spirit. Thus, after being born again, while we occupy the position of a son, if we fail to be shaped, mentored, and groomed by God the Father through the leading of the Holy Spirit, our condition will remain unchanged.

You might think that's a good thing. After all, in Malachi 3:6 God states, "I am the Lord, I do not change" – once saved, always saved. However, you are mistaken. Salvation/sonship is a free gift of God, but it does have relational expectations, which left undone by the recipient, signal to God that either the relationship is no longer desired or an unhealthy birth occurred.

> *"For God so loved the world that He gave His only begotten Son, that whoever believes in Him should not perish but have everlasting life. For God did not send His Son into the world to condemn the world, but that the world through Him might be saved. – John 3:16-17*

> *"The Spirit of the LORD is upon Me, because He has anointed Me to preach the gospel to the poor; He has sent Me to heal the brokenhearted, to proclaim liberty to the captives and recovery of sight to the blind, to set at liberty those who are oppressed; to proclaim the acceptable year of the LORD." – Luke 4:18-19*

> *But when He saw the multitudes, He was moved with compassion for them, because they were weary and scattered, like sheep having no shepherd. – Matthew 9:36*

If you have ever had the opportunity to observe the interactions between a father and son who enjoy a healthy and loving relationship with one another, several things will become very clear. Sons do not compete with their fathers in an effort to show them up or make them look bad. Sons enjoy assisting their fathers, and sons take pride in their ability to be useful or helpful to their fathers.

When considering the three passages of scriptures above, we see very clearly that Christ's agenda was established by His Father. God loved the world and predestined His Son to die for humanity's sin and be reconciled back to Him. Christ's only focus was to successfully complete that mission.

The scriptures record that Jesus faithfully died in our place, not out of obligation, but because He loved us, and seeing our condition, He was moved with compassion. He did not seek to promote His own agenda above God's, even when Satan offered Him that opportunity in the wilderness. Instead, Christ's singular focus was that of representing His Father's wishes to the world. Christ identified Himself so closely with God that He stated, "I and My Father are one" (John 10:30).

Sonship Exemplified

An examination of the scriptures will reveal that not only did Christ obey the wishes of His Father, indeed, He exemplified sonship. His relationship with His Father is characterized by the following:

- Sharing the work of His Father – John 5:19; 9:4; 10:37
- Knowing the Father and His will – John 4:22-23; 6:45-47; 8:55; 15:15
- Sharing in all that the Father had – John 16:15
- Enjoying special access / influence with the Father – John 14:13-16
- Demonstrating love for the Father – John 4:31
- Receiving love from the Father – John 3:35; 5:20; 10:17; 17:23
- Receiving all things from the Father – John 3:35; 13:3

Sonship and Discipline

So how does God discipline His sons? The scriptures provide us insight in the methods He uses to develop His spiritual children into sons.

God's Methods of Discipline

Method	Description	Scripture Reference
Tests	A season of personal turmoil that reveals your spiritual character to you	2 Corinthians 13:5
Trials	A season of personal turmoil that produces an aspect of spiritual character (e.g. patience)	James 1:3, 1 Peter 1:6-7
Rebuke	Sharp, verbal correction; used to produce immediate response	1 Timothy 5:20, Titus 1:3; 2:5
Correction	Re-teaching or training for the purpose of instruction; type of re-alignment	2 Timothy 3:16
Disfellowship	Removal from fellowship with the community of faith with the hope that the one being cast out will repent	1 Corinthians 5:1-5; 9-11

The Traits of Sons
- Faith
- Forgiveness
- Friendly
- Fun
- Focus

Sons

- **Are faithful to their fathers** (Titus 1:4, 1 Timothy 1:2) – "To Titus, a true son"; "To Timothy, a true son"
- **Resemble their fathers** (1 Corinthians 4:17) – "For this reason I have sent Timothy to you, who is my beloved and faithful son in the Lord, who will remind you of my ways in Christ."
- **Encourage their fathers** (2 Corinthians 7:13) – "Therefore we have been comforted in your comfort. And we rejoiced exceedingly more for the joy of Titus, because his spirit has been refreshed by you all."
- **Comfort their fathers** (2 Corinthians 7:6) – "Nevertheless God, who comforts the downcast, comforted us by the coming of Titus…"
- **Labor with their fathers** (1 Thessalonians 3:2) – "…and sent Timothy, our brother and minister of God, and our fellow laborer in the gospel…"

The Benefits of Sonship
- Abundant Life – John 10:10
- Eternal Life – Matthew 13:43
- Inheritance – Romans 8:16-17

Summary

While in the natural the word 'son' refers to a male child, in the Kingdom of God, it refers to any believer who has been born again by the Holy Spirit, has begun the process of spiritual development, and has committed to the local ministry to which he/she has been called.

Sonship is the covenantal term used to describe the relationship that exists between these believers and God the Father. When we become sons, we also become joint heirs with Christ. We must use the model of His relationship with the Father as our example of the epitome of spiritual sonship.

There is a difference between church membership and being a spiritual son of your leader. While church members simply attend church, spiritual sons have definite characteistics. Which one are you?

How have you demonstrated faithfulness to your leader? (Titus 1:4, 1 Timothy 1:2) ❏ Yes ❏ No

In what ways do you resemble your leader? (1 Corinthians 4:17)

_____

_____

_____

_____

How do you encourage your leader? (2 Corinthians 7:13)

_____

_____

How do you comfort your leader? (2 Corinthians 7:6)

_____

_____

_____

In what areas do you labor with your leader? (1 Thessalonians 3:2)

_____

_____

_____

Looking at your answers above, are you exhibiting Kingdom sonship? After reviewing the above aspects of spiritual sonship, toward which two are you going to make more intentional efforts?

_____

_____

_____

_____

_____

_____

_____

_____

_____

_____

Chapter Nine:
The Seven Drivers of the
Kingdom in Action

1. Sovereignty

As a Kingdom citizen, we should embrace the sovereignty of God. When we declare Christ as Lord (Romans 10:9-10), we are embracing Him as our sovereign, master, Lord, and potentate. Therefore, a Kingdom citizen accepts these facts and realities about God and our life in relation to Him.

As a Kingdom citizen, we acquiesce to His wisdom, knowledge, and understanding. If God allows it to happen, then He knows best. So who are you to get offended by His ways or whatever He allows to be. We must embrace God's sovereignty even when we do not understand and even when it hurts us terribly. We must never get an attitude with God regardless of what happens in our lives, because we accept His sovereignty. We never leave our post of service, and we never lose our appreciation for who He is and how He is! Job teaches us to maintain our praise in the midst of loss, saying, "The Lord gave, and the Lord has taken away; Blessed be the name of the LORD" (Job 1:21).

God is in Total Control
As a Kingdom citizen, we understand that nothing can happen without the approval of God. Satan cannot attack you and me without the permission of God. The book of Job demonstrates this for us when Satan and the angels were asked to give an account of their whereabouts. Satan was allowed to assault Job only by the permission of God with restrictions. So, as a Kingdom citizen, we understand that Satan can only do what God allows him to do, and since that is a fact, it is not meant for our destruction, but for our development. Paul writes that when one is called to Kingdom purpose that all things are working together for the ultimate good of both God and the Kingdom citizen. Our King is faithful and just and has His subjects' best interest at heart. Thus, we must learn to trust our King!

Without Faith, it is Impossible to Please/Serve Him

As a Kingdom citizen, we must learn to trust God when we cannot trace Him. Since He is perfect in all His ways, and He is in total control, all things will work together for our good. We must trust God when things are bad and things are good. We must always remember that faith is not simply a mental disposition, but faith is an action based upon the Word of God. Faith must be in action! A Kingdom citizen always believes no matter what the situation is or what you are going through that God is somehow going to bring you out with a praise and a testimony!

So Kingdom citizens embrace the sovereignty of God that positions us to live a more enriched Kingdom life that touches other areas of our Kingdom walk.

2. Stewardship

As Kingdom citizens, we are called to a disciplined life of stewardship or the management of the financial affairs of our sovereign God. Kingdom citizens must embrace stewardship in the following areas:

Tithes and Offering

Every Kingdom citizen returns 10% of what God has allowed him/her to have. The tithe should be taken off the top or the first thing you take care of. The Kingdom citizen also participates in freewill offerings, which is a specified amount above the tithe.

Building Programs

The Kingdom citizen understands the importance of worship facilities and therefore participates in God's building program, much like the Old Testament saints participated in the building of the Tabernacle and the Temple.

Spiritual Gifts

Kingdom citizens strives for – first, identifying their spiritual gift, then using their spiritual gift to expand the Kingdom.

Stewardship is a Kingdom principle that must be embraced for the continual establishment of ministries that will impact the world for Christ. It is God's revenue generation program for His church and all Kingdom citizens participate in making the church a strong church, just like taxes make a nation strong.

3. Structure

As a Kingdom citizen that embraces the sovereignty of God, we must then embrace the structure of God. God's structure deals with His apostolic rule and order. The structure of God spells out who is to report to whom and how; it is the leadership span and order of the Kingdom. A Kingdom citizen understands that since the King Himself chooses His officers then to submit to His officers is to submit to the King Himself. So as a Kingdom citizen that embraces the structure of God, we must do the following:

As Kingdom citizens, we have learned that God chooses to work in an organized manner through hierarchical ranks. So every Kingdom citizen strives to be decent and in order (1 Corinthians 14:40). We endeavor to keep the faith in a manner that is pleasing to God, for He is not the author of confusion. Hence, as believers, we should always make every effort to maintain peace, especially in the environment of God. As citizens of the Kingdom, we obey the order of the house of God, we do things the way that the structure of the house or ministry that God has placed us in is designed. We do not buck the system, unless it is not a biblical system. And if we have a question about the way things are run or conducted in God's house, we must handle it in a respectful and biblical way. We must go to the leadership and discuss our concerns in a peaceful and spiritual manner, maintaining an open mind.

211

Acknowledge God's Leadership

As Kingdom citizens, we must recognize and respect those that God has placed in office (Ephesians 4:11). Kingdom citizens embrace the set leadership of God's house and ministry. We must stay in our lane and allow God's leaders to govern the house of God and the flock of God in the manner they choose.

Allow Leadership to Equip You for the Work of Ministry

We understand that it is the role of the five-fold ministry team to train, develop, and place us in ministry (Ephesians 4:12). We must serve where we are needed, not necessarily where we desire to serve, so that the body can be edified and grow. A Kingdom citizen serves where leadership needs them the most in order to supply support where support is most needed.

The structure of God allows us to be able to execute the Great Commission and take the gospel global. Kingdom citizens ought to desire to take the message of our King abroad!

4. Servanthood

As a Kingdom citizen, we not only embrace the sovereignty of God, structure of God, and submit to the structure as sons, but we also embrace servanthood. Kingdom citizens are called to be servants. Christ proclaims that he that is the greatest in the Kingdom is he that serves. As Kingdom citizens, we must live out the following:

Service in Ministry

We must serve in ministry. Every Kingdom citizen should be involved in at least one ministry responsibility in the local church. The Kingdom citizen's service to the local church allows Christ to expand the impact and influence of the Kingdom.

Service in Discipleship

We are called to participate in Kingdom discipleship. Every Kingdom citizen should be engaged in inviting people to Christ and worship, bringing people to worship and Christ, and compelling people to surrender their lives to Christ. This should take place in every setting in which the Kingdom citizen operates – work, community, etc.

Service in Missions

Kingdom citizens are called to expand the borders of the Kingdom globally. Everyone should be involved at some level in supporting global missions or in taking the gospel of the Kingdom from Jerusalem to the uttermost parts of the world.

Servanthood is essential to Kingdom living; Christ Himself came to serve; hence, you and I must live a life of service to the King and to those whom He is calling for salvation!

5. Sacrifice

As a Kingdom citizen, we must embrace sacrifice. Sacrifice is the heart of the Kingdom. It was the key that opened the gates and allowed us to enter. Every citizen that has benefited from the sacrifice of Christ understands the great necessity of living a life of sacrifice, so that others may enter into the Kingdom. Sacrifice in the life of the Kingdom citizen must take place by:

Self-denial

As Kingdom citizens, we are called to deny ourselves and pick up our cross. The Kingdom citizen places the life of the Kingdom above his own interests and concerns. It is a life marked by continual service unto the King and the world, at the expense of our personal endeavors.

Relinquishment of Material Things

Every Kingdom citizen understands that the Kingdom is of great worth and value and is willing to forgo material things for the sake of advancing the Kingdom. Attitudinally, we must relinquish in faith, aspiring to relate to our material possessions like Abraham related to Isaac.

Sacrifice of Praise

As a Kingdom citizen, we must live a life of continual praise (Hebrews 13:15). The Kingdom citizen summons the presence and power of God by offering God praise and thanksgiving in every situation.

The Kingdom citizen sacrifices himself – his time, talents, and treasure – for the expansion of the Kingdom!

6. Submission

As Kingdom citizens, we not only embrace the sovereignty and structure of God, we submit to the sovereignty and structure of God. While the Western world tends to struggle with the concept of submission, Kingdom citizens understand the great necessity of submission and the potential joys that are latent in submission. We must embrace submission as a lifestyle that allows us to participate in worship unto the King! The Kingdom citizen that embraces submission must engage in the following:

Submission to the Will of God

Kingdom citizens understand the imperativeness of submission. There can be no relationship with the King without submission. The Kingdom citizen submits to God through obedience to the Word of God in all situations. We understand that God's will has precedence over our desires.

Submission to Spiritual Leadership

Kingdom citizens understand that spiritual leadership represents God's spiritual authority upon the earth in His church and ministry. As Kingdom citizens, we both obey and submit to spiritual leadership, which is submission to God Himself. Submission is not simply doing what the leadership requests, but it is executing with a good attitude and understanding that this is God's structure in action. Submission involves obeying the Word so the believer is not commanded to submit to personal or carnal requests; submission is predicated upon the Word of God.

Submission to Headship

As Kingdom citizens, we understand that submission is ultimately to God, and when we submit to His structure and leadership, we are submitting to Him. Kingdom citizens embrace their roles in the church, family, and ministry. As a husband, you should be submitted to spiritual authority in the church (your pastor), and a wife should be submitted to spiritual authority in the home (your husband). The children should be submitted to the spiritual authority of their parents.

Submission is a very important driver of the Kingdom in that it is the pivotal place of worship and service. Without submission, Kingdom service cannot occur, thus it is not sincere worship in spirit and truth!

7. Sonship

As a Kingdom citizen, we understand and appreciate sonship. Kingdom citizens are placed in a position of honor as sons of the King. So as sons, we must reflect the following:

The DNA of Our Heavenly Father

We must reflect (manifest in our behavior) the fruit of the Spirit, not our temperaments or personality types. We must strive to reflect the lifestyle of Christ daily.

We should ask ourselves constantly "What Would Jesus Do?" in this situation and try to reflect His actions.

Rely on Our Father's Wisdom

As sons, we should allow the wisdom of our Father to prevail over what we think and desire. We must strive to be sons of obedience, which means we must constantly read and study the Word of God, so that we can understand the mind of our Father in our day-to-day situations.

Accept Correction

As Kingdom citizens, we embrace the reality that sons must undergo constant chastening and correction, which is not pleasurable, but necessary (Hebrews 12:8-11). Sons do not mind being put on the spot, challenged about their actions and attitudes, and chastened. Sonship is important, because it speaks of the intimate aspect of the relationship that the citizens have with God the King. The King not only rules over us, but also fathers us.

Summary

In a nutshell, Kingdom citizens embrace the sovereignty of God through accepting the fact that God is in total control. The God that is in total control has developed a structure through which He chooses to govern His people. This structure is the local church and its leadership, and as Kingdom citizens, we submit to that structure by submitting to the local church leadership. While we are called to submit to the structure of God, we can feel safe and secure due to the relationship that we have with God as sons who serve their heavenly Father faithfully as stewards that are willing to sacrifice to advance His cause!

Chapter Ten:
Kingdom Invitation

The Kingdom of God is made up of a multiple relationship structures; it provides the king and servant model (sovereignty, servanthood, stewardship), father and son model (sonship, structure, submission), and friend and brother model (servanthood, submission, sacrifice). Although the Kingdom of God is highly structured, it is first and foremost highly relational. Everything we do in the Kingdom is aimed at building strong Kingdom networks of relationships (Matthew 13:36-43).

These Kingdom principles are extremely important in order to understand your role and responsibility as a citizen operating in the Kingdom of God.

Jesus sums it up:

Then Jesus sent the multitude away and went into the house. And His disciples came to Him, saying, "Explain to us the parable of the tares of the field." He answered and said to them: "He who sows the good seed is the Son of Man. The field is the world, the good seeds are the sons of the kingdom, but the tares are the sons of the wicked one. The enemy who sowed them is the devil, the harvest is the end of the age, and the reapers are the angels. Therefore as the tares are gathered and burned in the fire, so it will be at the end of this age. The Son of Man will send out His angels, and they will gather out of His kingdom all things that offend, and those who practice lawlessness, and will cast them into the furnace of fire. There will be wailing and gnashing of teeth. Then the righteous will shine forth as the sun in the kingdom of their Father. He who has ears to hear, let him hear! – Matthew 13:36-43

Now when one of those who sat at the table with Him heard these things, he said to Him, "Blessed is he who shall eat bread in the kingdom of God!" Then He said to him, "A certain man gave a great supper and invited many, and sent his servant at supper time to say to those who were invited, 'Come, for all things are now ready.'

But they all with one accord began to make excuses. The first said to him, 'I have bought a piece of ground, and I must go and see it. I ask you to have me excused.' And another said, 'I have bought five yoke of oxen, and I am going to test them. I ask you to have me excused.' Still another said, 'I have married a wife, and therefore I cannot come.' So that servant came and reported these things to his master. Then the master of the house, being angry, said to his servant, 'Go out quickly into the streets and lanes of the city, and bring in here the poor and the maimed and the lame and the blind.' And the servant said, 'Master, it is done as you commanded, and still there is room.' Then the master said to the servant, 'Go out into the highways and hedges, and compel [them] to come in, that my house may be filled. For I say to you that none of those men who were invited shall taste my supper.' – Luke 14:15-24

This scripture aptly demonstrates the culture of the Kingdom: it is inviting and evangelistic. It teaches us that there were three summonses. Metaphorically, this portion of the parable refers to two categories of people. First, in its immediate context, it is talking about the Jews' invitation to the supper. They were the first invited guests. They were invited from the Old Testament to the New Testament. When the servant of God came, Jesus, and invited them they said, "We have no time for you." Next, it refers to a group called the church – those that are resting on their laurels, past accomplishments, and traditions. They are resting on the fact that they have tenure, and based on that, they think they are going to get in without having to come to the Master's banquet.

Note in verse 17 that the Master sent His servants (apostles) – whoever He sends has the power of attorney. It was like He himself said "Come", because the servant told them to come. He sent His slaves – people totally committed to the Master. This text is also talking about servants/slaves. The servant is a person that is intimately connected to the Master. The person that is guaranteed to be at the banquet is the servant. No one else is guaranteed to get a seat, but the servant.

All the dialogue that was taking place occurred between the servant and the master and no one outside the relationship.

Erchomai is the Greek term for "come." *Erchomai* is what we call in Greek a present imperative. Present tense means "habitual". So it means, "Come and keep coming; don't ever stop coming, and it is not an option. It is an imperative that you come." It is a mode of demand. When He went to the first group, He was saying, "Come, now is the time". Unfortunately, the master was ready, but the guests were not ready for the master. They were honored when they got invited, but when it is was time to come, they had issues. In verse 18, they all, on one accord, began to make excuses.

But the man had the mindset that the food would not go to waste, so if the people who were initially invited were not coming, He wanted to find someone who would come. For the 21st century person, this can refer to people who initially had a relationship with God, but backslid. Initially, they may have accepted the invitation, but when it was time to go to the banquet, they were preoccupied. In the same way, many people have forgotten their initial commitment to God, because they became too busy playing with their new things. The Bible says the deceitfulness of riches, the desire for other things, and the concerns and cares of this world come and choke out the word (Mark 4:18-19). The man had scheduled a banquet, but had no guests. So he now was angry and upset about the invitation that people refused to receive.

Jesus (the master of the supper) said that He would then extend His invitation to the 'not so popular', the poor who He knew would be excited about the invitation to His supper. These are people who know that something is missing and need fulfillment. The Bible says, "Blessed are they that do hunger and thirst after righteousness, for they shall be filled (Matthew 5:6). "Blessed are the poor in spirit, for theirs is the Kingdom of heaven" (Matthew 5:3).

The key to filling the banquet table was finding people who were hungry and wanted to eat at the table of the Master.

It was finding some people that understood that they needed more than they had to work with; the kind of people who were maimed and crippled and had been hurt by life's circumstances. The Master wanted people at His table and cared not about their ethnicity, race, class, etc. He needed somebody that could appreciate a good meal. Many people have walked out on Jesus. They have chosen to chase relationships, marriages, businesses, careers, etc. But what does it profit a man to gain the world and lose his soul? (Mark 8:36). Metaphorically, the second group represents the low-class Jews. The third group, the highways and hedges, represents Gentiles. For the Gentiles, He said, "compel them to come."

Therefore, we see that the three levels of evangelism are invite, bring, and compel. Compel means "to apply pressure or use influence, persuasion, or lock them in a corner and make them have to come." You have to become creative. As long as it is ethical, you may use any means to compel them, because the Master does not want an empty seat in His House!

The Master does not care how you look, because He has a new wardrobe for you. You can come just as you are. The King has already pre-tailored a royal robe of righteousness for you. The Kingdom servant should be bringing people to the Master's house. Another group kept going and kept compelling. So evangelism is about inviting and compelling people to come to Christ. Christ is looking for people that have not accepted Him (unsaved), and He is looking for people that have accepted Him to go out and bring other people until the banquet hall – the embassy – is completely filled. When you are in ministry, there should not be an empty chair. When you walk in the embassy by yourself, you should feel convicted. The harvest is plentiful, but the laborers are few. The King is having a banquet. Who are you bringing?

Closing Remarks

I hope that you have been blessed and enlightened from the contents of this book, *Introduction to the Kingdom*. This book is the first of a multiple series of books designed to help believers understand the Kingdom – "A Journey to the Kingdom".

If you are really interested in learning the Bible through a Kingdom perspective and in its original context, consider the University of Dana Carson Ministries (UDCM). UDCM offers Kingdom training that provides a basic eight course program designed to teach the learner the basic tenets of theology. "Training For Reigning" is a program designed to teach both leaders and laity the fundamental concepts of the Kingdom through 12 courses that approach critical doctrinal tenets through the prism of the Kingdom. Also inquire about our Five-fold School of Ministry where we equip and train apostles, prophets, evangelists, pastors, and teachers. UDCM also has an online church health and growth institute that is designed to train pastors, leaders and key laity in principles of church growth and health through webinars. Lastly for those who desire to gain greater levels of financial literacy enroll in my online School of Financial Training, where you will learn about budgeting, banking, credit, investing, taxes, retirement, insurance, entrepreneurship, real-estate and much, much more from a Kingdom perspective! Thank you for your support of Dana Carson Kingdom Ministries. Please visit my website, www.drdanacarson.com, for my teaching and preaching Kingdom resources.

Keep your eyes open for my next Kingdom book coming soon!

About Dr. Dana Carson

As a Pastor

Dr. Dana Carson is the founder and senior pastor of the Reflections of Christ's Kingdom World Outreach International (The ROCK) in Alvin and Houston, TX. – a Bible-centered, Spirit-filled, Community-building, Kingdom-minded ministry founded in 2003. Dr. Carson has over 25 years of full time and pastoral ministry experience. Dr. Carson is one of the nation's foremost Kingdom theologians and down-to-earth pastors whose radical message and raw delivery are known all over the world. Dr. Carson's call and purpose is to educate people of every age with the message of the Kingdom of God that is both exegetically sound and spiritually nourishing. Dr. Carson has an exceptional concern for children and youth and personally invests his life in their training and development. Dr. Carson's anointing represents a combination of Spirit-filled fire and formal academic training, with a touch of the lessons learned in the ghettos of Chicago. With this rare anointing, he touches the hearts of people from all cultural, ethnic, and religious backgrounds worldwide.

As an Apostle With a Prophetic Voice

Holding firmly to the mandate in Matthew 28 that commissions all believers to go and teach all nations, Dr. Carson has planted and oversees Bible-centered, Spirit-filled, Community-building, Kingdom-minded leaders and churches worldwide. He has trained leaders and planted ROCK churches in New York, Louisiana, Dallas, Alvin, Austin, Elgin, and Lake Jackson, Texas as well as South Africa, Liberia, and the Philippines. Currently, Dr. Carson provides an apostolic covering for over 100 churches internationally. Dr Carson is a pastor's pastor with his profound pastoral insight and ministry experience. Dr. Carson has a heart and passion to train and equip pastors for the work of ministry.

Dr. Carson's desire to help pastors and young ministers was a result of a vow that he made God. When Dr. Carson began in ministry, as a first generation preacher and pastor, he was unable to get any assistance from seasoned pastors. So God sent him to seminary.

It was difficult, but so richly rewarding that he promised God that if He would provide him with a theological education, that he would commit his life providing mentorship to others who lacked spiritual covering and mentorship. Dr. Carson's training in theology (D.Min.), leadership (Ph.D.), counseling (C.Psy.D.), and business (GEMBA) have made him a rare and unique ministry gift and tool to the Body of Christ that continues to prepare both young and experienced pastors for sound biblical Kingdom ministry. Dr. Carson takes spiritual mentorship seriously by ensuring that he personally mentors all of his sons and daughters through the ministry of empowerment, apostolic infusion, and impartation. Dr. Carson has one of the most respected prophetic voices in South Africa and Liberia among the grassroot community and church leaders. Dr. Carson has spoken prophetically to nations and thousands have been healed, delivered, and made whole by the power of God. Through the demonstration of the Kingdom of God, blinded eyes have opened, the lame have walked, the dumb have spoken again, cancer and other diseases have been cancelled, and barren women have become mothers!

As a Community-Builder

Dr. Carson's fervor for lifting, developing, and building communities is second to none. Dr. Carson studied The Church and Economics and Community-Building during his doctoral studies at Harvard University. Dr. Carson wrote his dissertation on the relationship between African-American males between the ages of 14-35 and the independent church at Boston University, the alma mater of the distinguished Martin Luther King Jr. and C. Eric Linclon. Dr. Carson has been building communities through youth outreaches through athletics and academics for over two decades. He has created jobs and prepared countless numbers of people for employment opportunities through his many non-profit organizations.

Dr. Carson defied the odds by establishing a vibrant ministry in an unlikely place that continues to touch people in Brazoria County and the Greater Houston area.

The ROCK has served the Alvin community for years with health awareness fairs, Hurricane Katrina relief services (food, housing, employment assistance, and transportation), by providing Christmas gifts to underprivileged children through Operation Blessing, and mentorship and exposure opportunities through a federal at-risk program for junior high school youth. The ROCK helps to prepare Alvin children for academic achievement by giving away backpacks with school supplies and providing immunization information, while they enjoy giant inflatable fun, games, food, and entertainment through its annual Back 2 School Bash. Along with these community investments, Dr. Carson is a former president of the Alvin-Manvel Ministerial Alliance and serves as a chaplain with the Alvin Police Department. At the Reflections of Christ's Kingdom World Outreach Intl. (www.therockwoi.com), people of all ages, races, and backgrounds gather weekly to hear his electrifying, transforming teaching in an extraordinary worship context filled with interactive media technology.

As a Scholar

Dr. Carson holds three earned doctorates: Boston University in Theological Studies, specializing in church growth, Regent University in Organizational Leadership, and Logos University in Christian Psychology. He also holds three Masters degrees: a Master in Counseling and Guidance from Texas A&M, a Master of Divinity from Austin Presbyterian Theological Seminary/Oral Roberts University, and he was the first full-time clergy to ever graduate with a Global Executive MBA from the world-class Fuqua School of Business at Duke University. Dr. Carson's bachelor's degree in Business Administration is from the film location of "The Great Debaters" – HBCU Wiley College. His theological prowess and wisdom are also recognized in the academy. Dr. Carson presently serves as an adjunct professor of leadership in the doctoral program at Oral Roberts University.

The ministry's focus on the spiritual and educational empowerment of children and youth is birthed from Dr. Carson overcoming the odds of Chicago inner city living as a high school dropout. Yet despite dropping out of high school, he has unquestionably become one of the most scholarly and dynamic preachers of our time. He hopes that his life will inspire the next generation to become leaders in government, education, business, church, and family.

As an Entrepreneur

Dr. Carson is the youngest son of the late John and Geneva Carson, former sharecroppers from Mississippi, who instilled an astute entrepreneurial mindset to their baby boy. Dr. Carson is the Chief Executive Visionary and founder of Dana Carson Kingdom Ministries, Inc. (DCKM), a non-profit ministry organization designed to spread the gospel of the Kingdom while restoring families and communities through programs of empowerment.

Through DCKM, Dr. Carson spreads the good news of the Kingdom around the world. However, DCKM is only one of six small business units established to resource and support the expansion of God's Kingdom: DCKM Consulting, an organization dedicated to helping churches increase their membership and develop their administrative infrastructure; Carson Consulting Group; IntelliChurch Kingdom Products and Curricula; Kingdom Leaders Institute (KLI), an online Bible college for bivocational leaders that desire a firm foundation in biblical doctrine and ministerial training; and Brazoria County Athletic Association, an AAU division conducted out of the ROCK Fun and Fitness Center in Alvin, Texas. Over his 25 years in ministry, Dr. Carson has also established multiple day care and early learning centers and Christian schools for children ages 0-12.

As an Author and Seminar Host

Dr. Carson is a prolific author and writer of biblical study guides and curricula. Dr. Carson has written numerous books in theology, leadership, and church growth.

Dr. Carson has written multiple dissertations and thesis submitted to various academic institutions for the satisfaction of graduate letters from distinguished universities. He recently released *One True King*, the book sequel to the widely acclaimed *The Doors of the Church are Closed*. Other books from Dr. Carson includes *Incarnational Leadership, Kingdom Change and Transformation, and Lord Help! I'm Trapped in the Church*.

As a leadership scholar, Dr. Carson conducts professional leadership seminars to community, church, and business leaders worldwide. Dr. Carson is a trained counselor and therapist who hosts effective marriage seminars in ministries across the country. Dr. Carson is the founder and president of the University of DCM, which is aimed at training and developing laymen weekly through free Kingdom Bible studies. Dr. Carson is also the Chancellor of Kingdom Leaders Institute of Theological and Ministerial Training (KLI). KLI has been training pastors, leaders, and very serious laymen globally through this formal training institute for over five years.

As a Father and Husband

Dr. Carson is a devoted husband to First Lady Rachelle Carson, who serves faithfully in ministry with him. They have been blessed with five children, Dana Carson II, John Anthony Carson, Angel Naomi Carson, Marielle Alli Sanchez, and Devon Jarrod Carson. Dr. Carson loves spending time singing and playing sports (basketball) with his very talented and gifted children.

As an Evangelist and Revivalist

Renowned nationally, Dr. Carson ministers extensively through seminars, crusades, and television. His preaching and teaching has been broadcast on TBN, Daystar, the WORD Network, and primetime network TV. The DCKM broadcast can be viewed on StreamingFaith.com (Live on Sundays at 10AM and 6:30PM), LiveStream.com, and YouTube.com.

Combining biblical study and scholarship with the lessons learned in the ghettos of Chicago, Dr. Carson is frank and real – people love the way he teaches the practical application of the Word of God on a level that anyone and everyone can understand.

Renowned as a theologian, respected as an apostle, regarded as a prophet, an evangelist, a pastor, a teacher – he is the Man of God. He is God's appointed, He is God's anointed – sent by the King for such a time as this!

Additional Publications

One True King: Surrendering Our Attitudes at the Altar of Revival ISBN: 0-9780615387-9-5

The church of the Lord Jesus Christ is facing its finest and final hour - a Revival of unprecedented effectiveness! God is placing the church back into Kingdom alignment that we may experience power and authority like the contemporary world has never seen, as we submit our lives to His Lordship. This book will assist believers in making the Kingdom of God a reality in their lives and move them to the next dispensation of theologial awarness. This book is a must read fo the those who desire to fulfill the will of God in their lives.

The Doors of the Church are Closed
ISBN: 0- 97816047794-7-9

The Doors of the Church are Closed is one of the most relevant 21st centrury writings to the church. Statistics suggest that nearly 4,000 churches are closing with only 1,200 to 1,800 opening annualy. Less than 20% of Americans attend church and 97% of churches didn't win one convert last year! Yet, the church has exchanged its mission of the Kingdom expansion for popularity and wealth. The Doors of the Church are Closed! This book identifies the root causes of the contemporary church's failure and raises some monumental challenges to believers.

The Kingdom, the Church, and YOU!
Issuse That Impact the Lives of Every Believer
ISBN: 0-9746616-7-8

This book will revolutionize your thoughts concerning the Kingdom of God and its relationship to the church and how they mutually impact your walk with Jesus Christ.

The issues discussed in this book are very seldom discussed in church settings, but greatly impact your walk with Christ and with other believers. Dr. Carson, Dr. Young, and Dr. Grizzle provide insight on the Kingdom of God as scholars who are committed to the practical presentation and understanding of the Kingdom concerning modern cultural and theological issues. Your understanding of the Kingdom, the Church and YOU, will never be the same again!

Kingdom Change and Transformation
ISBN: 0-9746616-9-4

Research suggests that change is a very difficult process, and as a result, very few individuals ever change. Unfortunately, life and its design are structured for constant change; everything and everyone is in a constant state of flux, changing either for the best or for the worst. Dr. Carson explains, from a biblical and clinical perspective, why change is needed and how to practically employ change initiatives that will position you for greater levels of success. This book will teach you how to achieve the much needed and wanted change that you have earnestly pursued, possibly for years, but have been unable to achieve. This book will revolutionize your thought process as you learn how to think different and become a different Kingdom you!

Coming Soon!

Lord Help! I'm Trapped in the Church
Lord I Want to Be Big, But Little has Got Me!

Other Books By Dr. Dana Carson

Let's Get Real! How Total Transparency Can Transform Your Total Life ISBN: 0-97707389-4-6

Incarnational Leadership
ISBN 0-9746616-5-1